Digital Transformation
Center of Excellence

Fujitsu DXP Consulting

Keith D Swenson
Todd Palmer

Published by
Purple Hills Books
San Jose, California, USA

High Risk Activity
The Customer acknowledges and agrees that the Product is designed, developed and manufactured as contemplated for general use, including without limitation, general office use, personal use, household use, and ordinary industrial use, but is not designed, developed and manufactured as contemplated for use accompanying fatal risks or dangers that, unless extremely high safety is secured, could lead directly to death, personal injury, severe physical damage or other loss (hereinafter "High Safety Required Use"), including without limitation, nuclear reaction control in nuclear facility, aircraft flight control, air traffic control, mass transport control, medical life support system, missile launch control in weapon system. The Customer shall not use the Product without securing the sufficient safety required for the High Safety Required Use. In addition, Fujitsu (or other affiliate's name) shall not be liable against the Customer and/or any third party for any claims or damages arising in connection with the High Safety Required Use of the Product.

Contents

Contents

Chapter 1

COE Introduction

The purpose of any Center of Excellence is to strive to get to level 5 on the maturity model. The higher the level, the more effective the center is, and therefor the better return on investment. At level 1 action is chaotic and self defeating. The likelihood of getting high quality from a level 1 organization is small, and good releases are happen-chance depending on the circumstances of the particular release. Resources spend sometimes make a good return on the investment, and sometimes they don't. As you increase in level, the ability to produce regular, high quality releases increases. The investment made pays off more regularly, and everybody benefits.

In this book we use Capability Levels based on the OMG Business Process Maturity Model. A reasonable goal is to try to increase one level per year. You start by assessing your current level. Then work to attain the next level within a year, and within 5 years attaining the highest level.

1.1 Understanding The Center of Excellence

This section explains how to proceed to understand the documentation for the formation of the Center of Excellence and to understand the current state of the Center of Excellence.

1.1.1 Charter

1.1.2 Roadmap

The Roadmap provides a high level guide to the progress of the COE toward its readiness goals. The roadmap specifies activities and deadlines for the first year in the life cycle of the COE.

1.1.3 Methodology

The COE has a Methodology for designing, managing, and measuring Case Management projects. The methodology is in a constant state of development and improvement based on the experience the COE gains as it designs and implements new projects.

1.2 Capability Levels

The Capability Levels are based on the OMG Business Process Maturity Model.

1	Initial	wherein business processes are performed in inconsistent sometimes ad hoc ways with results that are difficult to predict.
2	Managed	wherein management stabilizes the work within local work units to ensure that it can be performed in a repeatable way that satisfies the workgroup's primary commitments. However, work units performing similar tasks may use different procedures.
3	Standardized	wherein common, standard processes are synthesized from best practices identified in the work groups and tailoring guidelines are provided for supporting different business needs. Standard processes provide an economy of scale and a foundation for learning from common measures and experience.
4	Predictable	wherein the capabilities enabled by standard processes are exploited and provided back into the work units. Process performance is managed statistically throughout the workflow to understand and control variation so that process outcomes can be predicted from intermediate states.
5	Innovating	wherein both proactive and opportunistic improvement actions seek innovations that can close gaps between the organization's current capability and the capability required to achieve its business objectives.

Chapter 2

Maturity Assessment

Every COE project should start with an assessment of the maturity of the current team, and that should be followed by yearly re-assessments until you meet your goal. It is so important to be able to report improvements in maturity, so that you have demonstrable evidence of the results of your hard work.

The assessment is used as a scorecard for regularly scheduled assessments. In general the scores are similar to the Capability Level. However, this is not a hard and fast rule. The assessment score should be treated as an internal measure that the COE uses for constant improvement. The criteria is defined over 15 measurable metrics over 7 sections.

2.1 Scoring

Each metric provides a score between 1 and 5. The lowest score for a particular metric is 1. Given there are 15 metrics the minimum score is 15. The maximum score is 75.

2.1.1 Metrics Scored In Sequence

A score of a metric can only be achieved if it can be shown that all of the lower scores for that metric are achieved. For example, you must evaluate whether the criteria for a score of 2 is successful before you can consider whether the criteria for a score of 3 has been met.

2.1.2 Partial Points

If the COE is making progress to the next point level in a metric, it can be considered for a partial half point. Hence the possible range of scores for a particular metric is the set defined as follows:

1.0, 1.5, 2.0, 2.5, 3.0, 3.5, 4.0, 4.5, 5.0

For example, in the Vision and Mission section the COE may be in the process of producing documentation and it is currently under review by the COE. In that case you could consider a score of 1.5 instead of just a score of 1.0.

2.2 Maturity Assessment

2.2.1 Foundation

The COE has a clear and specific Vision and Mission.

No document exists	1
Document exists but only for internal use.	2
Documented, reviewed, accepted and understood by the team of the COE.	3
Exists in a format that can be sent to customers.	4
Customers can easily find and read the document.	5

The Objectives of the COE are well documented and clearly communicated.

No document exists	1
Document exists but only for internal use.	2
Documented, reviewed, accepted and understood by the team of the COE.	3
Exists in a format that can be sent to customers.	4
Customers can easily find and read the document.	5

Does the COE have a mature Service Catalog that is readily available?

No document exists	1
Document exists but only for internal use.	2
Documented, reviewed, accepted and understood by the team of the COE.	3
Exists in a format that can be sent to customers.	4
Customers can easily find and read the document.	5

2.2.2 Governance

The COE is implementing a mature Governance Model that defines the organization and the operating model including funding and issue escalation.

No document exists	1
The COE is working with an ad-hoc governance model that at least defines the organizational structure of the COE with roles and task scope.	2
A structured Governance Model is in place that defines escalation, organizational alignment, funding, and change management.	3
The Governance Model has been shown to include effective change management and is providing measurable results.	4
A mature Governance Model is in place that is regularly reviewed and has been shown to work on multiple completed COE projects.	5

Does a Maturity Model Framework exist for assessing and progressing the capabilities of the COE?

No document exists.	1
COE has done some sort of capabilities assessment.	2
Maturity Assessment Model is Documented.	3
Regularly scheduled Maturity Assessments are taking place.	4
A plan is in place to rectify the Maturity Assessment short comings.	5

The Performance Measures (KPI) of the COE are well documented?

No document exists.	1
The COE has done some sort of Performance Measure Planning, such as draft documents.	2
Performance Measures are fully documented.	3
Regularly scheduled evaluations based on the Performance Measures are taking place.	4
A plan is in place to take action based on the metrics defined in the Performance Measures. Performance Measures have been used for evaluation of the COE after multiple projects.	5

2.2.3 Architecture And Design

The COE has a mature Solution Methodology in place.

No existing projects or Methodology.	1
COE has documented Methodology that is ready for use on COE projects.	2
The Solution Methodology has been used on at least one project.	3
A structure is in place for evaluating completed projects and has been used to assess the effectiveness of the Solution Methodology.	4
The Solution Methodology has been fully proven by using it in multiple successful projects.	5

2.2.4 Technology

The COE has a mature Technology Model. This defines the tools that are being used and how the stack of tools is being evaluated for appropriateness based on the objectives of the COE.

No Technology Model exists.	1
The existing technology stack is documented. This includes the tools that are in place and how they are used.	2
The COE has an approach for evaluating new technologies and understanding their impact on the Technology Model.	3
A complete Technology Model is in place an documented.	4
The Technology Model has been shown to be mature by leveraging it on multiple projects.	5

The COE has a mature Environment Management Model in place. This describes how new environments are stood up both at the development, testing, and production level

No existing model	1
COE has preliminary model describing environments for development, testing, and production.	2
The Model documents how to configure and deploy the covered environments.	3
The COE has a structure in place based on the Model for the efficient deployment of new environments.	4
The Model has been fully proven by using it in multiple successful projects.	5

2.2.5 Library And Asset Management

The COE has a mature Asset Management Model.

No existing Asset Management Model	1
All assets are stored in a central repository. This includes documentation and also project assets.	2
The COE has a documented strategy explaining what assets are stored where.	3
The COE has documented procedures that can be followed by new members explaining how they can find and update COE assets.	4
The COE has a complete Asset Management Model.	5

2.2.6 Project Management

The COE has a mature Project Management Model in place.

No existing projects	1
COE has completed at least one project.	2
A structure is in place for evaluating completed projects.	3
Multiple successful project completed and evaluated.	4
Multiple projects: the projects are documented and available for customers to browse.	5

The COE has a mature User Support Model in place.

No existing Readiness Model	1
The COE has documented the current state of skills training.	2
A plan is in place to enhance the readiness of the COE.	3
Team members are being trained according to the training plan. Current state and progress is documented. Readiness assessments are happening based on a documented schedule.	4
The COE has a team of members that have fulfilled training programs and have leveraged the training in actual successful projects.	5

2.2.7 Readiness And Training

The COE has a portfolio of successful Projects it can use as references for new projects?

No existing projects	1
COE has completed at least one project.	2
A structure is in place for evaluating completed projects.	3
Multiple successful project completed and evaluated.	4
Multiple projects: the projects are documented and available for customers to browse.	5

The COE has a mature Readiness Model in place.

No existing Readiness Model	1
The COE has documented the current state of skills training.	2
A plan is in place to enhance the readiness of the COE.	3
Team members are being trained according to the training plan. Current state and progress is documented. Readiness assessments are happening based on a documented schedule.	4
The COE has a team of members that have fulfilled training programs and have leveraged the training in actual successful projects.	5

2.2.8 Record Your Totals

Clear and specific Vision and Mission.	
Objectives well documented and clearly communicated.	
Service Catalog readily available?	
Governance Model that defines the organization and the operating model including funding and issue escalation.	
Maturity Model Framework exist for assessing and progressing the capabilities of the COE?	
Performance Measures (KPI) well documented?	
Solution Methodology in place.	
Technology Model in place.	
Environment Management Model in place.	
Asset Management Model.	
Project Management Model in place.	
User Support Model in place.	
Project Portfolio as references for new projects.	
Readiness Model in place	

Chapter 3

COE Capabilities

A digital transformation initiative is not just about making applications, but it is also about organizational change to adopt these new approaches. For this to succeed, a strong Center of Excellence is needed to facilitate the changes and to ensure the success of the teams adopting the new approach. This will mean growing in maturity, from a newly formed team, to a team that consistently delivers and supports other teams delivering projects.

This document outlines a suggested pattern for growing the maturity, and reaching a level 5 maturity within 3 years based on experience at Fujitsu and other sources.

3.1 Best Practice For Development Team Skills

This purpose of this chapter is to outline the proper skill set for a digital transformation development team of around 17 people.

The exact team needed will depend upon the precise requirements of the specific application, so this recommendation can only be a rough guide; however such projects do have enough in common that we can lay out some basic patterns

We work around the idea that the development team will be approximately 17 people, primarily because that is good size for a team that communicates well and can serve as an excellent example. In real life we often have to work with teams that smaller than that, and sometimes larger than that. These ideas can be scaled to match the team that is available.

We assume that the development team would like to develop with an Agile approach; using a set of goals, they will make a rough estimate of how long will be needed for the given team. The team will then be prepared to deliver at that specific point of time in the future. As a consequence, the precise functionality will not be known in advance. This allows for tight control of costs, but does not guarantee that any particular feature will be in the final product.

We assume that there is a short list of one or two applications that need developing right away to be the basis for forming the center of excellence around. One should never form a COE without an active project being worked on or delivered. If would be a mistake to first concentrate on forming the COE in isolation, and then only after that take on a development project. Such an approach would fall prey to false theories of how a project "should be" and has a tendency to design around unrealistic development patterns. It is only when you are actually struggling through the details of an existing project, that you realize the details of the various roles, and can make better assessments of trade-offs that are necessary.

3.1.1 Key Skills

Scrum Master / Project Manager   This person is keeping the project on course, making sure that the method is being practiced the right way. Most important, this person is addressing any organizational issues that come up to block the people on the team, making sure that every person has a clear set of goals and can work toward them.

Project Controller (PCO)   Represents the team to upper management, particularly for funding.

Software System Architect   This person is taking a larger view of the system being developed and makes sure that the system as a whole will function, and that it will fit well with the other systems that it must interact with. The architect must ensure that the solution will be robust. An architect may be specialized to a particular area, such as a security architect, or a specific technology such as SAP or .Net.

Architect Owner   a kind of business architect who works at creating and maintaining designs for the way that the organization works, separately from how they use the application being developed.

Process designer / business analyst   this is a person who has special skills in creating process diagrams that make sense and can also be executed. They will have experience in interviewing people to discover the business process. This person must know:

- BPMN – the specific way it is used by the product (Fujitsu DXP)

- Data modeling as needed in the process instance

- Java Action usage, which includes some need to know server-side JavaScript

- Timers and how to enforce deadlines with them

- Sub-processes

User Interface Designer   this is a person with skills in designing and implementing web pages. This includes: HTML, CSS, JavaScript, and a good understanding of how web pages are put together.

User Interface Programmer this is a person who is programming the interactions that a user will have with the web page, validating input, making panels appear or disappear as needed, updating values that have a calculated relationship between each other, sending the data to the server, maintaining and refreshing a cache of data on the client. This programmer works primarily in JavaScript, and should understand the working of the Document Object Model, along with one or more UI frameworks like AngularJS or React.

Integration Engineer this person understands how SOA work in principle and in practice. Both SOAP and ReST. The Integration Engineer probably works mostly in Java, but also web protocols, XML, JSON, and other web services style languages.

Database Engineer in most applications there is some need to read and write data to and from a SQL database.

Test Automation we expect most developers to write their own tests, but automating tests of the web GUI require skills that the average web UI designer or programmer doesn't have, so this person has that experience and knows how to create automated tests that would tell you right away if you broke something.

3.1.2 Skill Ratios

For a 17 person team, you might expect the following distribution of skills

(1)	Project Manager / Scrum Master. With this size team this is a full time job
(1)	Project Controller, generally not dedicated to one project
(1 – 3)	software architect / system architect
(1)	Business Architect / Architect Owner
(1 – 2)	process designers / business analysts
(4)	Web GUI designers (HTML, CSS)
(4)	Web GUI Programmers (JavaScript)
(1)	Integration Engineer
(1)	Database Engineer
(1-2)	Automated Test Programmers

3.1.3 External Skills And Relations

The following skills are provided by the organization as a service. The development team needs to have skills in these areas, but they also need to take steps to engage these external services to bring them in at the right time so that the project goes smoothly.

Database admin / architect   The development team will not be responsible long term for managing the data. That is the job of the db-admin team. It is normal for a db admin team to also have data architects who review and approve (and possibly even design) the data tables for a given application, so that they can be properly managed over the long term.

BPM Server Admin   the BPM / case application will be deployed to system admin group who will manage the BPM server for the long term. They will probably also set up the server.

Network Administration   every application must exist in a network which is managed centrally to assure that it runs, and to make sure that all the proper security features are in place.

Security Standards   Every organization will have someone who is responsible for the security of all applications, assuring that a consistent level of security precautions are present in every application.

3.2 Skills for Application Development

When you assume that the development is being done by external project teams, the question then becomes: how can a BPM center of excellence support those development teams?

3.2.1 Training

The most important thing is that the development team be properly prepared. This document will assume that the development team is properly prepared in standard programming practices:

- Java, C++, or C# development.

- SCRUM or other Agile method

- Test Driven Development techniques, testing frameworks

- Object Modeling Notation for diagramming

- Web page development (HTML, HTML5, CSS)

- Java Script programming (DOM, JS, JSON)

- Web servers, web protocols (HTTP, HTTPS)

- DevOPS practices of automating build, deployment, updating, etc.

- Standard performance and scalability techniques.

Beyond these, a COE should be prepared to deliver training on areas that are special to BPM, or sufficiently specialized that they should have specific attention on:

Web design for BPM applications. Do you create a single page application, or multiple pages, both are possible? What kinds of links will you be creating, particularly to enable the sending of email that refers to the application. Use of URL parameters. How to consistently leverage the Document Object Model (DOM) so that all applications are constructed in a consistent manner.

JavaScript framework for BPM Applications. How best to separate the visual view elements from the JavaScript object model. Common practices that make sense for BPM and case management applications.

The process client API. How information is represented in the BPM system. What information is held within the process, and what is outside the process. How to construct complex object (lists, maps, repeating structures). When to use XML, when to use JSON.

Process programming. BPMN diagrams. How prologues, epilogues, and role scripts work. Java Actions. Transactions, rollbacks, and compensations. Sub-processes, remote processes. How to find processes in error mode, and how to recover. Process versioning and process migration. How to define and use UDAs, including lists and maps. How the directory server (Active Directory) is leveraged for logging people in, and how it is used for defining groups. How to interface with the source management system properly and effectively.

Process and data management. How information is stored by the BPM server in the DMN and in the database (outside of the normal process information). How to interface documents with web pages to attach documents to processes. How to properly control access.

Process software administration. How to set up the BPM server, how to configure it. Control access to the server and to the tenants and applications installed on the server. Cluster management. Searching for and recovering from process errors. Transaction management. Extending the server with system wide Java Actions. Upgrading the server. Backing up and restoring the data for a server. Updating applications. Managing user groups and access to the applications.

Process integration. How to use java actions to access external web services and other services. What is available in the server enactment context (SEC), how to use it, and how to avoid problems.

The following three training areas are optional; however we have seen that maturity in this area greatly helps the team to succeed.

Error Reporting. Called out here as a separate skill because of how important it is in a DevOPS environment to have clear and accurate error reporting. As you integrate many services which are independently developed, there will always be situations where a change in one causes an unexpected situation in another. A clear message at run time can save immense amounts of time and effort in resolving the difficulty. There needs to be a clear path all the way from the problem to the user for details on what went wrong so that it can be addressed, and that might mean traversing multiple levels of servers and services until finally being displayed. Failure of one link in this chain cancels all benefits of reporting problems. It is important to use "Error First" approach.

Multi-user testing Techniques. We assume that developers are adept at testing single user applications, and multi-user non-collaborative application, but BPM and other collaborative applications are designed around people interacting with each other. When one person does one thing, it changes what another user sees. Some special techniques are needed so that you can test this style of interaction. Since BPM is about allocating work to specific people in flexible ways, there are many opportunities for "race-conditions" when multiple people try to do the same thing at the same time. Modern UI techniques tend to cache more state in the browser, which makes the window for such conflicts to be larger than dumb-terminal style applications.

Application Domain Partitioning. The World Wide Web functions as a well-connected information source even though all the information is not coming through a single data source. This allows the Internet to scale to immense size without limitation. The same should be true for large corporate BPM applications: You cannot (and should not) have all the cases hosted on a single server. Instead, the domain is partitioned and allocated to different servers. This partitioning should not be done arbitrarily, but instead according to patterns that optimize server use.

3.2.2 Training Across Roles

Some training is needed by all roles while other training might easily be taken only by a single role on the team. Here is a matrix showing preferred training of team members.

Symbols: * Key Skill, x Important to Know, . Could be useful, a blank means not important.

Training / Role	Mgr	Arc	Ana	GUI	JS	Data	Int	Tst
Web design	.	x		*	*			
JavaScript framework	.			x	*			
The BPM client API		x		x	*			.
BPM process	.	x	*	x		x	x	x
Data management		x	x			*		.
Server Administration	.	x				x	x	
Process Integration		x	.				*	
Optional:								
Error Reporting		x	.	x	x	x	x	x
Multi-user Testing		x	.		x		*	
Application Partitioning		*	.			.	.	x

Roles are: Scrum Master / Project Manager (Mgr), Software System Architect (Arc), Process Designer / Business Analyst (Ana), GUI Designer (GUI), GUI Programmers (JS), Database Engineer (Data), Integration Engineer (Int), Test Automation (Test).

3.2.3 Monitoring and Adapting

Training is up front, and possibly refreshed at a regular rate. Monitoring are steps taken to assure that the proper procedures are being applied. This should not be viewed so much as enforcement, but rather sharing of best practices in context. The real life problems faced by teams are never as simple as those presented in the training. The COE can provide Excellence beyond that given in training by helping to work through with specific difficult situations with the development team. This is a two way street. The COE can learn from the difficult situations, and take that back to improve the training. If certain situations are anticipated to be encountered more in the future, the training might be adapted to include those kinds of situations.

Process Diagram Review. There should be a step in the development process where the process diagrams are reviewed, including UDA and Java action usage, by someone from the COE who is an expert in process programming.

User Interface Code Review. Separate from the process review, individual parts of UI should be reviewed for conformance with usability standards, both on how they look and how a user interacts with them. Error reporting conforms to guidelines.

Security Review. Access control implementation at every stage of the application. Assuring that no data is delivered to the browser that user is not allowed to see. All the proper safeguards against hacking. Make sure that is transparent who does and does not have access to different things.

Testing Review. After the testing of an application is done, the results of the test need to be examined to make sure that all the special multi-user collaborative conflicts were properly tested for.

3.2.4 Talent Sourcing

Beyond training and monitoring, there are some skills that the COE might provide directly to the team. These consultants would be allocated directly to a development team, and work as part of the team for a period of time.

Process Architect. Needed mostly in the early 1/3 of the project, a BPM architect helps to make sure that the application is design will be effective in leveraging the benefits of a BPM server. This person might be freed up after development has started in earnest.

Testing Expert. This person joins the team in the latter half of the project and serves as a member of the test automation team, offering Excellence on how to test collaborative applications, stress, and scalability testing. The pool of individuals needs to be managed strategically in a way that is compatible with the needs and requirements that the organization and the future plans for application development.

3.2.5 User Support

Once the application is deployed into production, how do the users get help? We can presume that the standard pattern is that there will be a user support team for the individual applications. This might be accessed through a general help desk capability across the organization. The application support team will handle most of the issues which will be oriented toward the specific details of the application: what operations are available when, and what values go where. There will be times when the application enters a process state that the application support team will need help with. The COE is then there to help:

- Diagnose the process problem. What is the state of the process?

- Determine the source of the problem? Was the application at fault for allowing an incorrect action, or was it a correct action simply done at the wrong time.

- The problem can be rectified by manually resetting the process state to a different step in the process, or by manually updating a process UDA value, then escalate to the BPM Admin team to get this change accomplished.

- If the problem is an application defect, escalate to the application maintenance team for addressing.

- If the fault cannot be determined, escalate to the BPM vendor support team for help. The COE becomes the go-to point for solving runtime problems with process applications, and becomes the single point to contact the vendor or other outside resources.

3.3 Supporting Business Strategy

One key phrase best sums up the best practice in BPM: Don't pave the cow paths. BPM brings a new technological direction to the organization, one should not expect to work the same way as you have in the past. Because of this, the COE must be expected to work at the business strategy level to determine if the business is structured in the optimal way for a business process. Many of the functions of an organization are fixed by law or common practice, but many other aspects were simply selected years ago arbitrarily and have become entrenched. Taking advantage of the strategic opportunity of BPM requires questioning the basis for current practices, and seeing whether a better way might exist, aided by current technology.

- Goals for the COE. Can customer measurable goals be set? Such as every customer interaction is handled quickly and correctly. Can a more measurable form of this be adopted?

- KPI. Should the current ways of measuring performance be changed to better reflect the customer value?

- Awareness within the organization of BPM and case management

- Which BPM initiatives are important and how to prioritize among a set of such opportunities.

- What applications have been developed that can be reused with small modification for other purposes.

This responsibility is not centered in a single organization unit, and instead often spread across multiple units, so success in this area is about bringing multiple groups together and getting them to agree.

3.4 Guiding Infrastructure Development

The BPM systems must exist within the corporate infrastructure, which means that the COE must participate actively with the infrastructure groups to assure that the right capabilities needed for BPM are maintained.

The COE must work hard on organizational awareness and education. There are problems that are a good fit for BPM, and there are ones that are not. The organization as a wholes need to have enough of an understanding to distinguish which is which. Maintaining this general awareness will require regular high level training on the concepts.

Here is a list of artifacts maintained as available to the organization for this purpose:

- Very High Level "What is BPM" – single page description suitable for anyone, particularly non-technical audiences.

- General Developer Level BPM Architecture – 4 to 8 pages for general developer consumption

- General Administrator – for DB admins and other server admins who are not fully trained on BPM, but need to know a bit about it to coordinate their work with the BPM admins.

- BPM Analytics – a short, high level review of what is possible using BPM analytics. What kinds of measurements that might be able to be made.

The COE should also maintain a library of processes which have been used to use as examples and guides for future projects. Consistency of approach across project will make the infrastructure as a whole easier to maintain because it will be easier to reassign developers between projects.

3.5 References

http://www.redbooks.ibm.com/redpapers/pdfs/redp4898.pdf
http://www.bptrends.com/publicationfiles/FOUR

Chapter 4

Charter

The Digital Transformation Center of Excellence (DTCOE) aims to bring about new ways to improve business processes in order to provide better services for the organization.

You will generally need:

- Vision Statement

- Mission Statement

- Approach Statement

- Scope Statement

4.1 Vision Statement

A vision statement must be very short, something that can be reiterated quickly, and that people can grasp the meaning of very quickly. It is a statement of how the world might become. A vision statement, it describes the world beyond the organizational unit to include a vision of the containing organization, and even the city or region that the organization is embedded within.

Here is an example of a vision statement from an organization we worked with recently:

> The goal of any organization is to provide customers with complete and accurate business processes of any complexity that can be adapted quickly to all changing requirements.

Here is some analysis on the choice of the particular words in this statement.

provide customers – satisfying customers would be a goal of any organization. We normally thing of an organization providing goods and services, while the business processes remain in the background, almost as if they were an unimportant side effect. In truth, the business process is the thing that distinguishes between an organization that can delivery what the customer wants and one that does not.

complete and accurate – Organizations strive for quality in the way they work. What is a high quality process? It is one that accurately performs what the law or customs requires. The complete requirement and no superfluous requirement.

business process – The services are described as business process to reflect the vision all services can be best be offered and controlled as a process, even if that process is no known in advance.

any complexity – This is included to say that processes are not only simple predefined processes, but could be complex & unpredictable requiring case management techniques.

adapted – This is the agile approach. We all know that large complicated static business processes can become anchors that prevent progress when it is needed.

quickly − It is not enough that it is possible to change the process, but it must be possible to change the process easily, with a modest amount of resource, and without a lot of delay from any source.

changing requirement − The world is not static. It is a given that the rules of today will change. We do not desire change simple for its own sake, but instead change is a environmental factor we must deal with.

4.2 Mission Statement

The mission statement says who your customers are, what needs they have, and what you are going to do to meet those needs.

> The mission of the Center of Excellence is help process owners to define, improve, and optimize their processes to support personnel in meeting the ever-changing needs of the customer.

A significant part of this will be to train, guide, and help development teams to make the best use of BPM & Case Management technologies to create agile solutions more quickly and at lower cost. Here is some analysis on the choice of the particular words in this statement.

process owners – Not all processes are automated. The center of excellence can help define, measure, improve, and optimize processes even when not supported by a solution.

personnel – The solutions are software that is used by people to do their jobs.

ever changing needs – Reference to the need to be agile and that change is a natural requirement. This identifies those personnel as the customer of the development team.

the customer – The ultimate destination of the value being produced

train, guide, and help – The development teams are doing the work. What do they need to achieve the vision? Training will give them the skills. Guiding will provide leadership to show them the direction to head in, possibly coordinating between different groups. Helping is a catch all to fill in any missing capability directly as needed.

development teams – The primary customer of the center is development teams.

best use of . . . – There are many challenges that the development teams will face, but the one challenge that the center will focus on is that of how to leverage the potential of BPM and Case Management.

agile solutions – Solution is used here as the product of the development teams, and we want those solutions to be agile. We want to avoid large, rigid, and fragile solutions that cannot change.

4.3 Approach Statement

The approach to helping process owners will be to directly engage and provide services for measuring processes, evaluating efficiency, and suggesting optimizations.

> The approach to creating solutions will be custom development based on a powerful reliable development platform and reference architecture using an iterative agile method.

The approach to persuading development teams to do this will be through training courses, training materials, documentation, hands on help and guidance. The center of excellence will deliver such training, materials, and service.

Manual, non-automated processes, or partially automated processes, will be subject to process analysis by looking at what records exist of past process instances. This approach can be used to find bottlenecks and to determine the efficiency of the existing processes. From that suggestions can be made to improve the process, including possible automation.

The processes at any organization are unique in the sense that the specific requirements that the organization faces are not exactly the same anywhere else. This means that preexisting off the shelf solutions do not exist. The solutions must be custom developed, but one need not start completely from basic programming principles.

An agile approach to development is the goal of the center of excellence. Remember however that this is a goal for the development teams, so the Center of Excellence must employ a number of techniques to encourage agile development in the development teams.

The agile approach depends upon rapid implementation of small part of the project which are developed to the point of deliverable quality. This is the hardest thing to learn. An engineer naturally wants to have everything laid out first, and to then assemble in a single job. The false intuition is that software is like a huge machine, and that opening up the machine to do work takes time and effort. And closing up the machine after making the change is extra effort. Therefore, try to do as much as possible in a single time. But software is a design process, and it is not like a machine at all. It takes no effort to access any part of a body of software. Because of this, it is entirely reasonable to make a very small change at a time. And then to do the rest of the work around that change to make sure that it is

The approach is detailed in the Development Methodology documentation: Methodology-Agile-BPM-Implementation.docx, Methodology-Designing-Human-Processes.docx, Methodology-Persisting-Complex-Data.docx, and Methodology-Task-Assignment-Strategies.docx.

4.4 Scope Statement

The center of excellence services and material in a number of areas:

Methodology – An important part of doing business processes correctly is to take a consistent effective approach. center of excellence will provide methodology documentation and training courses on how to design, measure, run, and optimize business processes.

Process Method, Design Method, Data Method, Activity Method, others.

Process Maturity Assessment – Assessment metric definitions and tools for assessing maturity in process management.

Solution Architecture – Provide a reference architecture upon which to base developed solutions, and reviews of implementations as they proceed to assure appropriate conformance.

Case Management Platform – Technology to support BPM and Case Management will be provided and supported by the center of excellence including a process developer studio and process runtime environments.

center of excellence also serves as the path to support for any issues during development.

Glossary – Supporting consistent terminology throughout the projects.

Skills Training Materials and training on a variety of subject:

- Process Design
- Solution Development
- Process Administration
- Security Architecture
- User Interface Design and Interfacing
- Analytics and Reporting

Pilot Projects – Three solutions will be developed directly by the center of excellence as a way of proving the approach and demonstrating success to the rest of the organization.

Project Audits – Review of processes for process owners, and review of solution development projects in order to increase the quality and performance.

Project Assistance – center of excellence will provide process designers or business analysts to assist projects when needed.

4.5 Meetings

- Daily stand-up SCRUM meeting at 9:30 every working day

- Weekly meetings on subjects of importance that includes members from other centers.

- Potential bi-weekly and on-demand follow-up meetings as needed.

Chapter 5

A Methodology For Designing Human BPM Processes

The way you draw a process diagram depends largely on the methodology you use to define the process, as well as the underlying technology that you are going to use to implement the process. That begs the question then: what is the methodology for human processes?

5.1 What Is A Human Activity?

Before we talk about a method for drawing up human processes, we need to be clear about what a human activity is. Clearly it is work that is done by a human. This is not work that is done by a computer on behalf of a user. In order to focus on the human activity, we have to ignore all of the things that are done to facilitate that work. Or rather, we need to consider those things that facilitate the work, as part of the task itself.

When modeling human activity, we focus on the work to be done: wash the dishes, feed the dog, write the blog entry, and decide the menu for dinner. Naturally, for a group of people to coordinate on these tasks, there must be communications between them, but we don't model the communications. If I want my son to wash the car, clearly I have to tell him that I want him to wash the car, but I don't think of that as a separate activity in itself. Instead, it is part of getting the car washed.

It should not come as a surprise that systems designed for supporting human activities allow you to model the work that is to be done at every step in a process, without worrying about how you will tell that person to do the work, or how the results are collected. Such systems often include customizable ways that each user can decide how they wish to be informed: some users prefer email, others like to receive an SMS message on their phone, etc. As a process designer, I want to focus on the task to be done (e.g. review this document) and should let the system take care of how that user is informed about the work to be done. Similarly, I know that an activity may be concluded with a decision (e.g. to either "accept" or "reject" the document), and that may affect the path that the process takes, but I do not want to be too concerned at the high level of how the system collected that response.

5.2 Identifying Human Work

There are three reasons why an activity must be performed by a human.

First consider some cases there are decisions to be made that cannot be automated and must be made by a person. For example, the determination of whether an article is fit for publication is a task that depends upon recent current events, suitability of the writing style, and the editorial preferences of a particular publication. Another example, the decision of which candidate is the best fit for an open position is a task that depends upon personalities of the candidate and the team they would join, as well as an assessment of skills and ability to perform the job. These decisions must be performed by a person because the most relevant attributes may not be able to be expressed in a quantitative way, like political correctness or personality. The rule behind what constitutes acceptable quantities of these is tacit and is not consciously known by the people who evaluate such rules. But indeed there are people who are very good at making such decisions. This is work that will never be automated.

The second category of tasks is those which might one day be automated, but to do so would require additional prep work which has not been done. For example, you might need someone to enter figures from a financial report which is received either on paper or in an electronic format that is not easily consumable. For the time being, it is simply less expensive to pay someone to do this than it is to pay a programmer to write the code that automatically converts the information. Eventually, these will be automated.

The third category consists of physical tasks that must be done outside an information system. For example driving a forklift to load goods from a truck into a place in a warehouse. Or to perform maintenance on a piece of equipment. It might be possible in the far future to automate these tasks with robots, but there are significant barriers to automation due to the physicality of the task. For the time being, we must treat these as human work.

These human tasks are made explicit so that people with the right skills can be identified, or so that people can be trained to do those tasks. Everyone involved in the process needs to know what they do—not just those performing the task—so that everyone gains an understanding of how the tasks they do fits in with what the others are doing. The human tasks need to be described in a way that the people themselves will understand using the specific vocabulary that the people in that organization use. There will normally need to be additional documentation associated that contains detailed information that is useful for training or skills identification.

5.3 Meeting Human Needs

Before anyone will perform a task, they certainly must be

(a) informed that the task needs to be done,

(b) given the details of the particular case,

(c) able to do the work, and

(d) have a way to record the results of the activity.

These are part of any human activity. The human task facilitation system (Human BPM system) should provide those automatically as part of the activity node. That is to say, when a node is assigned to someone, and that node becomes active, it should send notification to the assignee, provide a way that the assignee can log in and access the details of the case, and provide a set of choices as well as ways to update the case data as appropriate for that process.

Besides the above required aspects of a human activity above, for practical reasons many human facilitation systems include the concept of a

(e) deadline date for an activity, as well as

(f) reminders about the activity and warnings that a deadline is approaching. These are convenient built-in capabilities to help manage the work.

So keep in mind that a human activity is a description of actual human work to be done, and that each activity is assumed to have (a) notification, (b) information, (d) conclusion, (e) deadline, and (f) reminders built-in. The following 9 step method can be used to create a model of a human process:

5.4 Step 1: Identify Human Work

Start by enumerating the tasks that must be done by people. List the work that is to be done by a person.

Ignore for the moment the paper form, the data on the form, or how that form is passed around. Do not think about email messages or ways that you might communicate about the work. Do not consider how web services will be accessed or updated. A common mistake is for system designers to jump to focus on the artifacts that help people coordinate their work, instead of the work itself.

Avoid including activities which do not involve humans. For example, running query on a database is something that might be need at some point in order to support a human task. At this point in the method you simply assume that the right information is available. There is a later step that defines what information must be available, and a final step that defines how that information is retrieved, but those should be defined at the right point, which is much later in the method.

5.5 Step 2: Determine Activity Conclusions

Human tasks can be concluded in more than one way. For example, the decision of whether to "accept" or "reject" an article for publication will be concluded in two ways: "accept" or "reject". The conclusion of an activity is an explicit part of the activity itself. In many situations, there may be a third conclusion to this example activity which is something that means more or less "I am not qualified to make this decision". That is a possible way that an activity might be concluded. Some activities will have acceptable time limits, and may be concluded simply by the passing of time. Each conclusion is given a name.

Conclusions are important communication events. When you model a human process, you are modeling thing that need to be communicated to the people involved in the process. Take for example the process of writing a book where many people are involved in various roles such as writer, reviewer, editor, etc. The writer will at some point declare that the book (a particular draft) is ready for review. While this concludes one phase of writing, more importantly it tells others that they may start their activities of reviewing and editing the current copy. The conclusion of a human activity is most often a speech act known as a "declaration". A declaration is a statement that in the act of uttering it, changes the state of a group of people. Declarations often redefine what many people are expected to be doing. So it is with a modeled human process: the completion of one activity redefines what other people in the process are expected to do.

A conclusion should be considered a distinct conclusion only if it matters to the group. Take for example a task "Answer Question". You might think of the answer to the question, as being the conclusion of the activity, and there are approximately and there is one (or more) answers to every possible question that might be placed. Clearly it is non-sense to consider every possible answer as a possible conclusion of the activity. Conclusions are grouped into sets which will affect the flow of the process further on. To be specific, if the flow of the process does not depend at all on whether the task is completed or not, then it is sufficient to say that there is only one conclusion: "done". The president is given the choice to "sign" or "veto" a piece of legislation, and the process continues in different directions depending upon how this task is concluded. However, there is a time limit, and if congress dismisses before the bill is signed, then this situation is called a "pocket veto". A "pocket veto" is considered to be completely identical to a "veto" as far as the process is concerned, so we would not need a separate conclusion for pocket veto: the timeout rule would simply be another way to conclude the activity as a normal "veto".

5.6 Step 3: Put The Tasks Into Order

The work and conclusions should be identified without getting overly involved in the sequence of activities. In many cases it is clear that a
particular task needs to be done before or after another related task.
There will also be branches, and certain tasks that are done only on certain conditions. This is where a diagramming tool becomes useful, but
only if it can describe activities at the human level. If one activity must
be completed before another, and that other activity can start as soon
as the first is completed, then an arrow is drawn between them.

If an activity can be concluded in more than one way, and if each
conclusion would cause the process to proceed in a different direction,
then there can be an arrow coming out of that activity for each possible
conclusion. Clearly, if the point of an activity is to "accept" or "reject"
an article for publication, the process that continues after that point will
be very different. Because this decision is the very point of the activity, the process becomes easier to read if there is a direct connection
between the activity and the direction that the process goes. Some engines can not represent this in this way, and instead save the conclusion
into a variable which is then tested at a following branch gateway. This is
an accepted and common practice, but because the branch is removed
from the human task, it is harder to see the direct causal link.

The result is a network diagram of the human activities that must be
performed properly set in a process which indicates the conditions and
order of the activities.

5.7 Step 4: Determine Performers

After the tasks and order are identified, one needs to determine who should do the tasks. This is highly dependent upon a particular organization. It is also changes from case to case. In some cases, there will be a pool of people who would be qualified to do the task, and anyone from that pool might be picked. What must be determined at this point is what set of rules will be used to determine who should do a particular job. It might be that a person with a particular skill is needed, and if a directory exists that lists all the people with that skill, then the rule is to find those people and pick one. More often the requirement will be that a particular person is chosen because of their responsibility in a particular part of the organization. For example, there may be a person designated to handle requests from a particular customer. Of there may be a person who is designated as handling all the purchase requests for a particular department.

Unfortunately such a rule cannot be specified without specific consideration of the organization that will be using the process. Each organization will have unique organizing principles, some of which are based on historical accidents. Even across a single organization, the rules to determine who does a particular activity may not be consistent. Any organization that grew by mergers of other organizations will have some "special" parts of the organization that are not like other parts. There also needs to be consideration about the specific representation of the organization in an organizational directory. If skills are not tracked, then that cannot be used to determine the person to perform the activity.

There generally will need to be an expression of some sort which can be evaluated in the context of the organization structure that resolves the assignee of a particular task. This expression will usually make use of pre-existing groups and/or job titles in the organizational directory. It may require new groups or job titles. There may need to be multiple levels of groups which include groups which include groups. In some cases it may not be possible to determine a priori who will be performing a particular task. In some cases the assignee expression will narrow it down to a group of people, but immediate circumstances (e.g. who is available) may be necessary select the final assignee. It might be necessary for the users to self-select for a particular job. There may need to be case by case adjustments, since it is not possible to know everything in advance.

5.8 Step 5: Determine The Information Model.

Here you specify a schema or a set of schemas which carry the information context within which all the activities take place. If the process is for a customer to open a bank account, then there is specific information that needs to be carried for that process, such as the customer name, address, and references to other accounts or credit history. The context schema needs to be a superset of all information needed for every activity. For example, if there is an activity to assess the property value of a house, then clearly the details about the home address, prior sales information, and various reports about the locale are necessary to perform this activity. If one activity produces a result which is necessary in a later activity, such as the assessed value of a house, then there much be a variable that will hold that information between activities. By considering the information requirements of every activity in the process, you can compile a complete context schema required by the process.

The information content will be modeled differently by different implementation engines. For some there is a single schema for the context that is shared by all activities (effectively a union of all schemas required by the individual activities). Others have a collection of schemas which are transformed back and forth through the process. Either way, the idea at this point is to identify the information requirements of the entire process.

5.9 Step 6: Define Access To Information Needed At Each Activity

At some points in the process, certain parts (variables) within the shared context can be read and updated and at other points that information can be read, but not updated. There are also points in the process where information is completely hidden because it is either not yet specified at that point in the process, or not relevant to that particular activity.

5.10 Step 7: Determine Timeouts

An activity may have a requirement to be performed in a particular time period. What happens when that time period is exceeded? Does the process continue without the activity being complete, or does the process "fail" and go down a different path. There may be reminders that are additional notifications to the user that the task has not yet been completed. There may also be escalation to other people or management if the task is nearing the deadline without being completed. At this point for each activity, all time-dependent behaviors should be considered. Some tasks may have no time dependency at all, and may be allowed to remain uncompleted indefinitely.

We know that time equals money; so it is worth considering at this point the cost of every activity, as well as the cost to the organization of either delaying the activity, or not performing that activity. If you are simulating the execution of the process, these costs entered into the model can be acumulated across a simulation run in order to guide the further design of the process.

5.11 Step 8: Design The Presentation Of The Information.

This puts a face on the context information, mapping the schema to a visual presentation. This presentation might be specific to a given activity, or might be the same presentation over the entire process.

Humans don't read XML directly. Instead, the information has to be displayed in a way that is meaningful to the user. To be effective, the display should be organized for ease of use. Some of the information may be keys or links to other information, and the display should provide an easy way to access those external sources of information.

Technology to present the information is often described as "forms" in the BPM community, but you should keep in mind that any technology that can take data and generate a user interface can be used. The choice will depend on many factors outside the BPM system. Some organizations will choose Visual Basic or Java Swing because they have programmers experienced in these areas. Some might choose PHP or other web technique. They might have a powerful forms software designed specifically for this purpose. The process definition method should not get bogged down at this point in the specific requirements of the technology to be used. Instead, this step should focus on the look and feel of the displayed information.

5.12 Step 9: Integrate To Information Services

This is where the information needed in a process can be picked up from various sources and sent to various destinations. I use the term "service" in the generic sense of a "Service Oriented Architecture" (SOA). This might be through "web service" calls or any other means to access other service types. The point simply is that there is a human activity that needs a particular piece of information, and so this is where you specify how that information will be retrieved for that human user.

It is this step where you finally consider how data is sent and received between computers. Many process designers start by considering how data is transferred through the system, and it leads them to a communications centric view of the work. It can lead to activities that are optimized for computer communications, instead of being optimized for human work. Since the human costs far outweigh the compute resource costs in most business processes, it is important to start with the human tasks, and then work down to the integration tasks.

To access information from a web service, some of the process context information will need to be transformed appropriately into XML that is needed as input to a web service. The resulting XML may need to be similarly transformed to be put back into the process context. For example, if a in an account application, the process may need to access a "credit rating" service to retrieve the applicants credit rating for consideration in the application process.

Services are used not only for retrieval of information; it is also the point where you consider how the results of the human tasks will be sent out to destinations outside of the people directly involved in the process. For example if the decision is made to approve a loan of a particular amount to a customer, then there are various parties that may need to be informed about this decision (e.g. by email) and there would also be calls to services to actually set up the account and initiate the sending of a contract to the parties involved.

5.13 Roles And Responsibility For Modeling

The business analyst and the developer take the modeling through the entire process. The modeling starts with the business side, and migrates to the technical side of the course of modeling. Different skills are needed at different phases, and these tend to be enabled or aided by people with those specialized skills. The table in figure 5.1 shows who needs to be involved at each step, and how the main responsibility tends to shift from business analyst to developer right around step 5.

	BA	U	M	DA	SE	UX	SO	D
1. Tasks	X	X						
2. Outcomes	X	X						
3. Order	X							
4. Performers	X		X		X			
5. Info Design	X			X				X
6. Access Control			X		X			X
7. Durations			X		X			X
8. Presentation	X					X		X
9. Integration							X	X

Figure 5.1: Responsibilities of role by stage: Business Analyst (BA), Users (U), Management (M), Data Architect (DA), Security Expert (SE), User Experience Expert (UX), SOA Expert (SO), Developer (D)

5.14 Summary

Nine steps lead to a model of a human process. The steps are repeated iteratively, with reviews at various points. Usually after each step there is some segment of the organization that are interested in reviewing the progress. It is also true that later steps will turn up details which were left out of earlier steps, and so there is some iteration through the method multiple times. A good system will allow simplistic execution of the process before you are complete, so that you can try out the process along the way. After step 3 you should be able to run simulations of the process in order to gain confidence on the correctness of the process. After the process is implemented and deployed, you can collect statistics on how well it is running and cycle back through this to improve things. We call it "Business Process Management" because you are never completely finished designing the process. This method is repeated as long as the process can be improved, and there are always new ideas on how to improve the process or to respond to external changes.

Chapter 6

Agile Process Driven Solution Implementation

This chapter describes an Agile approach to developing projects based on Fujitsu DXP.

6.1 Philosophy

There are two driving philosophies that are the foundation of this approach:

AGILE	We want to get something working quickly even with minimal functionality. This helps us understand what we know and what we don't know about the solution. Design flaws will be discovered early while they can still be corrected.
VISIBLE	Throughout the development of the solution we will be reviewing and validating a live system with the User community. This gives the Users a true understanding of the system and exposes misunderstandings. The system itself becomes the focal point instead of documents about the system.

6.2 Solution Implementation Phases

The following diagram provides an overview of the phases of the Agile Implementation Methodology.

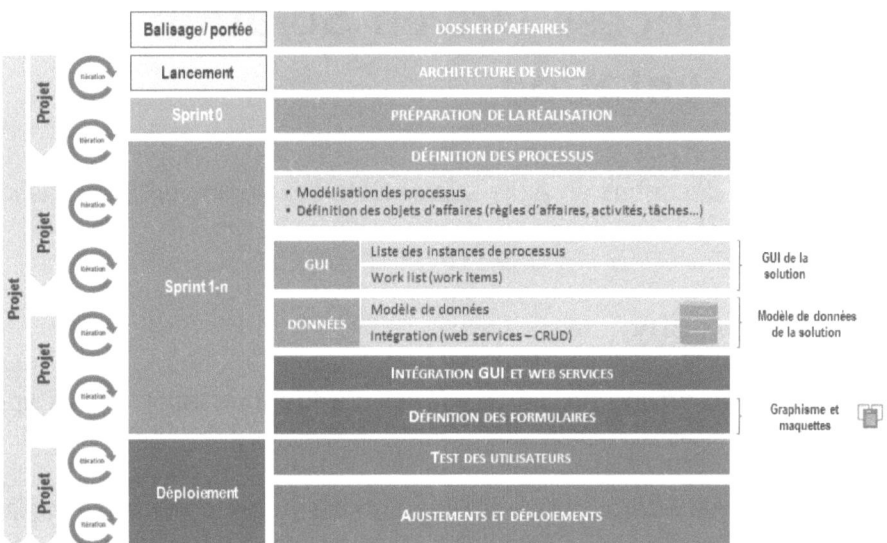

For this approach you can think of the implementation in the following phases. Note they will overlap.

1. Understand the Process

2. Process Design

3. Custom User Interface

4. Data

5. User Interface and Forms

6. Integration

7. Testing

In this chapter we will try to relate the concepts presented in concrete way using concrete examples. Even though this won't be a complete implementation of any process, it will still allow us to practice what we learn in the methodology.

6.3 Understand The Process

Artifacts

- Document

- Process Maps (Visio diagrams)

Activities

1. Identify the Managed Object

2. Identify the Processes

3. Define the MO high level properties

Documents

1. Methodology-Designing-Human-Processes.docx (Steps 1, 2, and 3)

In this phase we work closely with the Business Unit to document and understand important aspects about the process that will help us later when creating the solution.

6.3.1 Identify The Managed Object

First identify the main object that will be managed by the processes in the solution. For example, in a purchasing solution you may be managing Purchase Orders. In a customer support solution the object would most likely be Support Incidents. For the rest of this document we will refer to this main object as the *Managed Object* or MO.

Example

- In a purchasing solution you may be managing Purchase Orders.

- In a customer support solution the object would most likely be Support Incidents.

One Managed Object

For now you should resist the urge to say there are multiple managed objects. Typically, the Managed Object may come in multiple types. Or, those other objects are just parts of the MO or they be objects that are referenced by the MO.

Example

- A call center would have a Business Object of Call. There may be multiple types of the Call such as Complaint, Inquiry, or Contact. The Call Managed Object would have parts such as the Contents of the call. Finally, the Call Managed Object will reference other objects such as Customers or Product which are not Managed Objects.

If you find that you actually have multiple Managed Objects that are handled completely differently, you should consider choosing one to first move forward with. This is in line with an Agile approach of focusing on specific features and implementing them before moving on to add new features. Also, you should be able to treat these two Business Objects separately with completely different processes. Choosing which to move forward with is a decision that must be made with the Business Unit after discussing priorities and resources.

Managed Object Types

Managed Objects may come in different types. Note these types. The specific name of the MO is critical. This name must be verified with the

Business Unit. Also, the names of the specific types must be exactly defined and documented.

Example

- In our Call Center the Business Unit may refer to a Call as a Contact or Ticket or an Issue. Whatever the BU calls it should be used as the name of the Managed Object.

6.3.2 Identify The Processes

Once you have identified the MO, decide on the main processes that will actually manage the MO. In the Purchasing Solution example you may have a Handle Purchase Order process. These processes may or may not already be mapped out in something like Visio for example.

Example

- In a Purchasing Solution you may have a Handle Purchase Order process.

- In a Call Center you may have a process called Respond to Inquiry.

At this point when identifying the process, don't think in terms of process definitions. At this point you typically only need to specify one process. Most likely, the process will actually include multiple process definitions when we implement it in Interstage Studio.

Process Stages

Take a top down approach to understanding your process. Start by thinking about the stages that the MO goes through. For example, the MO may start out as pending, then be verified, and then either approved or rejected. Each stage will be a group of activities.

Example

- A Business Object like Request may go through the following stages: Pending, Verified, Approved or Rejected, Complete

- Each of these stages will then be expressed as the Status of the Request Business Object.

This has the following benefits:

- The high level process will be obvious.

- People new to the process will be able to easily understand the process.

- This will facilitate the use of sub-processes.

The exact names of these stages are also very important. Verify them with the Business Unit to confirm that they actually use those stage names when they discuss their MO.

Starting The Process

Consider how the actual Process Instance will be started. The following questions will help you to begin thinking in the right direction:

- Will the process be started automatically by an event in another system?

- Will it be started manually?

- Is it handled differently depending on how it is started?

- Are only specific people allowed to start the process manually?

Priority

Fujitsu DXP has the concept of Priority. Priority is available at the task level and at the process level. In DXP you can sort and filter Process Instances and Work Items based on priority. Here are some questions you can use with the Business Unit:

- Should certain Activities be completed before other others even if the others are older?

- Are there situations where certain processes are more urgent than others.

- Have you already defined specific prioties?

6.3.3 Define High Level Mo Properties

Start mapping out some of the properties of the Object. At this point you don't need an Entity Relationship diagram or anything like that. At this point in the project we won't have enough detail to justify an ER diagram. Just define a set of properties and a short description of them. For example:

Example

- Name: A string that contains the name of the requestor.

- Cost: A number in dollars that estimates the cost of the project.

- Department: The name of the department handling the request.

We will need to be able to uniquely identify each MO. So, each MO will need a unique ID. Usually, it is possible to use either the row number from the MO Database or the Process Instance ID. However, sometimes the Business Unit may already have an ID method in place. This ID may use something like date or type to construct it.

6.3.4 Examples

For complaints, Customers contact Revenue Quebec with Requests (in French: Demande). The Complaints Department (DTP) manages the Request. This customer request may be a complaint, providing information, or a suggestion. Each request may consist of multiple Reasons (in French: Motif).

Based on this we note that the MO is the Request. Even though we have Customers and Reasons, the Request is the top level object. Customers are not the MO because we don't access the customer except in the case of a request. Reason is not the MO because we don't have a reason without its parent request.

The main process we are interested in is Request Management. This is the process to manage a request from when it is created through its life cycle to being handled and closed. For now we define some high level MO properties:

- Customer: The information about the customer that has filed the Request

- Description: A high level description of the Request.

- Reasons: A set of Reasons the Customer is making this request.

- Type: The type of the Request. Note: we need some possible values for this.

6.3.5 Checklist

❑ You have determined the Managed Object (MO).

❑ You have a specific name for the MO and you have verified it with the Business Unit.

❑ You have documented the different types of the MO.

❑ You have identified the main process.

❑ The process has high level Stages defined and the names of these stages have been verified with the Business Unit.

❑ You understand the different ways the process will be started.

❑ The MO has a list of high level properties.

❑ Each MO property has a description.

6.4 Process Design

Artifacts

- Process Definitions (XPDL files)[1]

- Decision Tables (.dt files)

Activities

1. Design process definitions

2. Implement Business Rules

3. Test process definitions in Console

Documents

- Methodology-Designing-Human-Processes.docx

- Methodology-Task-Assignment-Strategies.docx

The goal of this phase is to get a Process Definition that you can actually step through in Console and see it working. This phase also addresses the implementation of Business Rules. Although, from the viewpoint of process design it is better to think of Business Rules as just another part of the process and not as something separate.

6.4.1 Design Process Definitions

This section follows the high level steps from the chapter section 5 A Methodology For Designing Human BPM Processes on page 41. You should be familiar with those concepts before proceeding with this section. Here are some high level guideline for designing processes:

- In general fewer process definitions is better. For now, avoid the temptation to create a lot of small granular Sub-process Process Definitions.

- At this point don't try to add any integration into the process. If you need data from an external system, hardcode it or enter it manually.

---

[1] XPDL format is an open standard for storing BPMN diagrams supported by more than 80 process tools. Business Process Incubator offers an open cloud-based converter for XPDL to other formats. BPMN format files are less universal. Since Interstage BPM uses XPDL internally it is most convenient to use XPDL for storing process diagrams.

Lay Out The Process

This section includes the following items from Methodology-Designing-Human-Processes.docx:

- Step 1: Identify Human Work

- Step 2: Put the Tasks into Order

- Step 3: Determine Activity Conclusions

Sometimes it helps to use a white board or Post It notes at this point. For now just focus on including the human activities. Once you have the general shape of the process laid out, start creating the Process Definitions in Studio. You can add place holders for integration points but don't implement anything with these yet. You may add things like condition nodes for well defined automated branches.

Make sure all your node names are unique within a single Process Definition (P360). Use the Process Outline View in Studio to check this. This is because a Process Instance that has two nodes with the same name can't be migrated.

Choices: Arrows from an Activity

Choices are arrows that have an Activity as there start point. It is important to remember that when the user "makes a choice" only one of these arrows will be activated and that it completes that activity.

Usually, you should avoid situations where an Activity has only one Choice and then goes directly to a condition node. Often, the user is making the decision in the form and the condition is just following that decision. In this case you should just have the user make the choice in the Activity by placing multiple choice arrows.

It is a good idea to also give the arrows unique names within scope of a Process Definition. This is because the arrow names are displayed in the process history. Unique arrow names help to avoid confusion in the process history. Also, the name of the Choice name should be descriptive of the action in the current task. Typically, you will want Choice names to be a verb stating the specific choice. Finally, don't use Choice names like "to management".

Example

- Good names for choices: Approve, Reject, Escalate, Veto, Submit, Next, Back, Withdraw

- Bad names for choices: Approved, Rejected, To Management, Arrow1, Exit

---

Roles And Assignees

This section includes the following items from Methodology-Designing-Human-Processes.docx:

- Step 4: Determine Performers

Swim lanes in Interstage are purely for documentation. Adding a Swim Lane doesn't change how the Process Definition functions. Hence, Swim Lanes are not mandatory. The benefit of Swim Lanes is that they can sometimes add clarity to the process. However, the downside is that they force you into a linear structure for laying out your activities that can sometimes make a simple process seem complex. Before adding Swim Lanes consider if the extra work and confined structure will actually add value.

UDAs

This section includes the following items from Methodology-Designing-Human-Processes.docx:

- Step 5: Determine the Information Model

Name

- This is the display name of the UDA.

- The Name should be what is most often shown to end users. As Revenue Quebec user interfaces will be in French the Name should be in French and can contain French characters.

- The Name can contain spaces

Identifier

- The Identifier must be unique in the Process Definition.

- Valid values follow the same constraints as programming languages. That is: it must start with an ASCII letter and not contain spaces or special characters.

- UDAs that start with an underscore "_" will never be displayed in the GUI.

Type

- The UI uses the type to know how to format the display of the UDA value. So when choosing the type consider what the display will look like to the user.

- For JSON date: use STRING UDAs

- Use XML UDAs only for communicating with SOAP Web Services.

- True/False or Yes/No should be BOOLEAN.

Hint: One good practice to identify the UDAs needed for a process instance is to mock up the user interface forms. Keep in mind that this is too early to really define the real UI. You need to identify the data fields before you design the UI, however we tend to think about data in terms of a form style layout with all the the fields on particular spots on the page, and we think about people entering these values and interacting with them. The purpose of the UDAs is just to support the forms that you are going to create. So preliminary mocks ups of the forms will allow you to think clearly about the data you need, and ultimately the UDAs that you need.

Worklist Udas

Determine which UDAs must be Worklist UDAs. Worklist UDAs are returned by the Interstage Server when the user fetches Worklist. Consider the following when deciding whether to specify that a UDA is a worklist UDA.

- contain information the user should be able to see in the worklist without having to go through the step of clicking on or opening the Work Item.

- slightly increase the load time of the worklist as more data must be sent to the client.

- should be small.

- Note: If you want to use a UDA to filter or sort Work Items, it must be a Worklist UDA.

For Worklist UDAs with of type DATE or BOOLEAN, add the type as a suffix to identifier of the UDA. This is because later in the Custom UI we will want to display these UDAs in read only format on the work list. For performance the Interstage server sends these Work List Work Items with only the Identifier and the value. Typically, in the Custom GUI we want to display Dates and Booleans with special formatting. This suffix tells the Custom GUI how to format these UDAs.

Example

- Name: Often marked as worklist UDA because we want to be able to sort and filter the work list by the name.

- Cost: We want to be able to display the Cost in a column in the Work List.

- RequestID: We want to be able to search for the ID of the Request.

Creating Udas

When creating UDAs always click on the Show Identifier Checkbox so you can actually see the UDA Identifier.

Typically, there will be multiple types of the MO. So, create a STRING UDA for the MO Type with the name of the MO with a suffix of Type. So for our Request example you will create a UDA with Identifier: RequestType. Typically, this UDA will be marked as a Worklist UDA.

Example

- So for our Request example you would create a UDA with Identifier: RequestType.

You will almost always want a Status UDA. This will be a STRING UDA with a specific set of possible values. These values represent the states that the MO can move through like: Draft, Pending, Approved, and Closed. Ask the Solution Owner what state the MO can be in throughout its life. Finally, the Status UDA should be a Worklist UDA.

Timers

Process level timers versus Activity timers and using an Activity timer as a process level timer.

Process level due dates versus Activity level due dates.

This section includes the following items from Methodology-Designing-Human-Processes.docx:

- Step 7: Determine Timeouts

An activity can have at most one due date. The main purpose of the due date is to specify when the task is overdue. A due date is specified by a timer. A due date timer doesn't actually need any BPM Action associated with it as the timer expiring automatically has the action of specifying that the activity is overdue.

Timers should almost always have at least one Action associated with them.

Typical situations for timers are:

- We want to send an email to someone to remind them that the due date is approaching.

- We want to re-assign the task after it exceeds its due date.

- We want to periodically increase the priority of a task.

BPM Actions

Add actions to update the Status UDA values.

By default the when a Process Instance is started it takes the same name as that of the Process Definition. This results in many Process Instances that all have the same name. Hence, you should typically use a BPM Action to set the name of the Process Instance based on some UDA value. For example, you could put the customer or request type in the name of the Process Instance.

Sub-Processes

Sub-processes in BPM can either add complexity or help to manage complexity. So, it is important to use them wisely. If you aren't sure whether you need to use a sub-process, you should avoid adding one. For purposes of discussion we will refer to the process that invokes the sub-process as the Parent process.

Deciding on when to use a sub-process can often be more art than science. Here are some good reasons to use a sub-process:

- You have a large process with many nodes. Breaking up the process into smaller sections can help performance and make a complex process easier to understand.

- Part of the process is managed by another group but is used in this process. For example: contract review.

- A part of the process is used by multiple types of the MO but in different ways.

- Part of the process needs to be iterated in parallel.

To reiterate: you should only use a sub-process if you have a compelling reason to do so.

Sub-process Versions

It is important to realize which version of the Process Definition gets invoked when a Sub-process Node is activated. The sub-process will be invoked on the Published version of the Process Definition at runtime. If there is no Published version, it will be the latest Draft version.

Hence, when you are publishing a new version of a Process Definition that is invoked from other processes you need to understand how this will affect those Process Definitions.

If you want to publish a new Process Definition version and do not want it to be invoked by currently running processes, there are a few approaches you can take:

- Create a new version of the Parent Process Definition and select Use the same subprocess definition version on the process properties. Migrate your existing Process Instances to this new version. The Parent Process Instances will continue to use the sub-process with the matching version number.

- Instead of creating a new version of the sub-process, you can save a new copy of the sub-process Process Definition as a new name.

This will be treated as a separate process and won't be linked to the current Process Instances. Finally, when you are creating a new Process Definition you should consider whether you want to tightly couple the version of the Parent process with the version of the sub-process by selecting: Use the same subprocess definition version. Even if you end up choosing incorrectly, you can always migrate the process Instances later to correct the situation.

Start Nodes

When thinking about starting a process you need to consider when you actually want the Process Instance to come into being. Let's review a few items before Proceeding. Note that a Start Node can have forms. Activating the Start Node cause a new Process Instance to start. Except in cases of dealing with errors you never re-activate or circle back to the Start Node.

You need consider when you actually need a Process Instance to be created and you should only start a Process Instance when you actually need one. For example, if a user goes to a web form to start a new request, typically the Process Instance should only be started after the form is submitted. If the user partially fills out the form and then cancels, there is no reason to start a Process Instance because you don't need to record this cancellation.

Chained Process

Chained Processes are often as sub-processes. But, it is better to think of them in terms of a completely new Process Instance that is started by an existing process.

One of the most common ways to use a Chained Process is for follow-up processing. At the end of a process you can use a Chained Process to handle review and follow up tasks. This allows the main process to complete and then the time that the follow up takes doesn't affect analytics or timers on the main process.

Voting Nodes

Of course the typical scenario for a Voting Node is to implement a voting scenario. However, in any situation where you need multiple users working on the same Activity you can also use it. For example, document review is like a voting scenario.

For the Voting Option, you typically want to leave the default so it uses *Evaluate voting rules on every vote*. Don't change this unless you have a compelling reason to make everyone in the role vote before evaluating the completion.

Finally, you can use a timer with a Make Choice Action to provide a default choice after a certain amount of time.

When to use evaluate after every vote

Iteration and when to use it: Compare to Voting node (Voting node each individual user does one task, iteration the same user could possibly do all the tasks)

Exit Nodes

It is typical and often useful to have multiple Exit nodes. In the case of multiple Exit Nodes you should name them with the result of the process or the state of the MO. As mentioned before, always make sure very node in your process has a unique name including Exit Nodes.

And Nodes

Remember that And Nodes will wait for an event on every incoming branch before proceeding. Hence, you need to assure that each incoming branch will eventually generate and event.

A possible error is that you can have branches for an exclusive choice node coming into an And node.

Useful Scenarios

This section explains scenarios in designing process where it may not be obvious how to implement the desired process behavior.

Deactivating Nodes

Process Designers are often in a situation where they need to deactivate an active node without actually completing it. The main way to deactivate a Node is to activate an Exit Node. However, you may ask how can I activate an Exit Node and still keep my Process Instance running. This is where the Compound Node is very useful.

Assume I have a situation where I have two Activities running in parallel: A and B. Activity B has two choices: Both and Skip. When the user selects Both we want to wait for both A and B to be completed. However, if the user chooses Skip I don't want to wait for Activity A to complete. The diagram shows how a Compound Node can be used to implement this scenario.

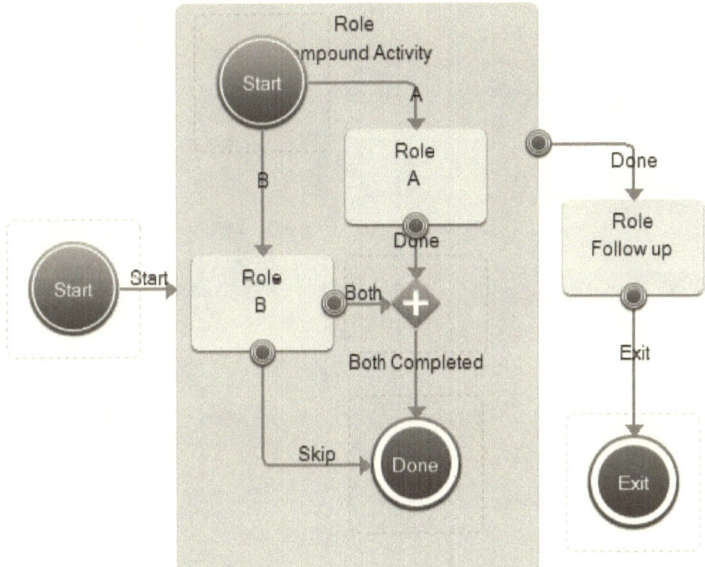

Non-exclusive Conditional Branches

Typically, a Process Definition will look much simpler than a Visio Flow Chart. However, non-exclusive conditional branching is one of the situations where the Process Definition is more complex than the Visio Flow Chart. Part of the reason for this is that Flow Charts can get away with a certain amount of ambiguity in the splitting and merging of parallel paths.

Condition Nodes are exclusive choices. This means that a single Condition Node evaluates to a single result. Hence, if you have multiple possible results, you use a Condition Node for each of them.

Notice that after the branches there is an And Node as we want to merge the branches before we actually proceed. We also need an arrow that skips the subprocess. This makes sure that the arrow send an event the And Node.

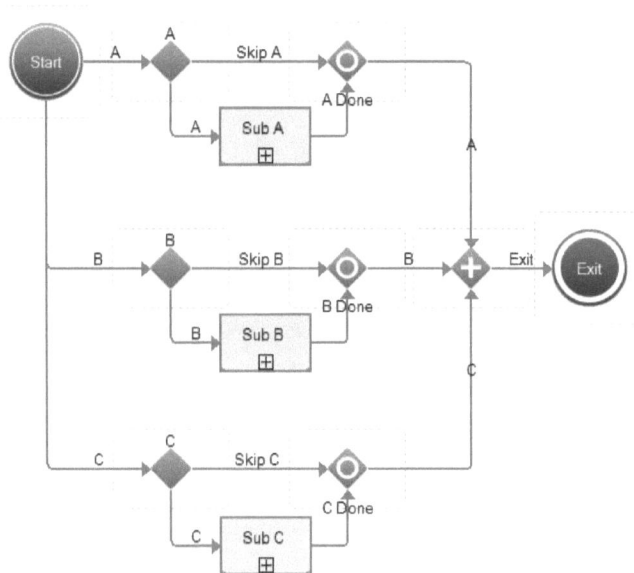

6.4.2 Business Rules: Conditions And Decision Tables

For purposes of the Methodology a Business Rule is anytime the system makes the decision instead of a person. This decision can be a path the process takes or it can just be information that gets added to the process.

When you think of implementing Business Rules in Interstage don't only consider Decision Tables. Often, a Business Rule can be more easily implemented using Conditional and Complex Conditional Nodes. Just because you are implementing a Business Rule doesn't mean you need to use a Decision Table.

For simple Business Rules you will typically use a Conditional Node. When implementing a complex Business Rule you will typically use a combination of Condition Nodes and a Decision Table.

Business Rules Toolkit

For implementing Business Rules you have the following tools at your disposal:

Conditional Node	• Designed to be simple to use.
	• Input: a single UDA
	• It compares the input UDA to a set of pre-defined constants.
	• Chooses one branch.
Complex Conditional Node	• Designed to be flexible enough to handle complex expressions.
	• Input: multiple UDAs and perdefined vales
	• Evaluates a set of expressions.
	• Chooses one branch

Decision Table	• Designed to handle multiple conditions for each result. • Input: Values from multiple UDAs. • Action: Compares multiple UDAs to a set of predefined constants. • Outputs multiple data values
Subprocess	• Invoke an existing Process Definition from a Parent Process. • Make a Business Rule reusable by wrapping it in a sub-process. • Should inlcude only items only items specific to the Business Rule. • Include one Exit Node for each possible result

Analyzing Business Rules

To assist you in analyzing Business Rules use the Business Rules Worksheet:

• Methodology-Business-Rules-Specification.xlsx

In the worksheet you will find the following questions that are useful for Analyzing Business Rules. The Worksheet includes descriptions and also guidance about how to implement the Business Rules based on the responses to the questions.

• What are the inputs?

• What are the possible results?

• Do any results have multiple conditions?

- Can the condition thresholds be determined at design time?

- Are the results exclusive?

- Are we only returning data or controlling process flow?

- Is this rule used in multiple places?

6.4.3 Test Process Definitions In Interstage Console

The goal is to get to a point where you are using and testing the Process in Interstage Console. Step through the Process Definition with the user community where they can see the choices and the consequences of choices in the process. This should create questions and discussions that require the Process Definition to be modified. Also, it will help to clarify the prioritization of features of the solution. Note we will still make changes to the Process Definition throughout the later phases of the implementation.

6.4.4 Process Definition Checklist

☐ Each node in the Process Definition has a unique name.

☐ Each arrow in the Process Definition has a unique name.

☐ The Process Definition includes a Status UDA.

☐ The Status UDA is being updated by BPM Actions.

☐ You have considered whether you want the Process Definition to be linked to the specific versions of Sub-processes.

☐ You have stepped through the Process Definitions in BPM Console with the Business Unit.

6.5 Custom User Interface

Artifacts

- Web Pages (html files)

- Cascading Style Sheets (.css files)

- JavaScript (.js files)

Activities

1. Create basic Interstage solution Custom User Interface

2. Test Process Definitions in Custom UI

In this phase we create a User Interface specifically for the solution. We will call this the Custom User Interface or CUI.

6.5.1 Create Basic Custom User Interface

The COE should provide a Custom User Interface template implementation. This simple Web Application can be used as a base and extended to create your own Custom User Interface.

Start with a simple user interface specific for the solution, but that is still rather generic. This custom UI uses the Interstage Agile Adapter Web Services to query the Interstage Server. It displays the process information to users in a web interface. This UI will typically have at least two Views: Process Instance List and Work Item List.

Process Instance List   This is the list of process instances. At this stage in the development you typically have one main Process Instance for each MO.

Work Item List   This is the task list of the logged user. It shows the list of Work Items assigned to the user. At this phase, when the user clicks on the Work Item it displays a default form with information about the Work Item. Later we will discuss forms which are the specific interface shown for an Activity.

6.5.2 Modify Custom User Interface

Modify the Custom User Interface that you created based on the Custom User Interface Template. This is where you add content that is specific to your application. For example add things like the name of the solution. Add sorting and filtering based on some of the Worklist UDAs. Consider changing the name of the Process Instance list to the name of your MO. Change the New Process Instance tab to something like "New MO_Name."

6.5.3 Test Process Definitions In Custom Ui

At this point the Custom UI displays only a generic form for each activity. This forms just shows some activity information such as the name of the activity and also the list of UDAs and their values. Again step through the Process Definition with the user community, but this time instead of using Interstage Console you will use the Custom UI.

6.5.4 User Interface Checklist

❏ The Custom UI has a Worklist.

❏ The Custom UI has a Process Instance list.

❏ You can manually start Process Instances from the Custom User Interface.

❏ The Worklist can be sorted and filtered.

❏ The Custom UI is checked into TFS.

❏ You have validated the Custom UI with the Business Unit.

6.6 Data

Artifacts

- Database Schema

- Web Services

Activities

1. Define Entity Relationships for the MO.

2. Create MO repository.

3. Create CRUD Services for the MO repository.

4. Modify the Process Definition to reference the MO instead of contain it.

5. Modify Custom UI to use the MO Services.

Documents

- Methodology-Designing-Human-Processes.docx "Step 5"

- Methodology-Persisting-Complex-Data.docx

This section deals with transitioning from the Managed Object being stored in the UDAs of the process to a more production ready approach where the MO is stored in its own application repository.

6.6.1 Define MO Entity Relationships

Specify exactly what the MO looks like. This includes the properties and their types. It also includes relationships to other objects. Typically, this looks like an Entity Relationship (ER) diagram for the MO. The ER Diagram can then be used to create the DB for storage of the MO.

6.6.2 Create MO Repository

Create a repository specifically for the solution. Typically, this will be a database that stores the MO and its related objects. Process information is stored in the Interstage database.

Sometimes the MO Repository may already exist. In some ways this makes the solution easier but in other ways it can make it more difficult is the repository can't be modified. For example, in a Process Driven solution we typically want to track the Status of the object. If the current MO Repository doesn't already have this it will need to be added. If it can't be added, then another database specifically for the solution is needed. In this additional repository you store only the extra information for the MO that isn't already in the MO repository.

6.6.3 MO Services

In this phase we implement the Create/Read/Update/Delete (CRUD) Web Services for the MO. These Web Services provide interaction between the application and the MO Repository.

It is preferable that these will be REST based Web Services rather than SOAP. One of the main reasons for this is that REST Web Services typically return a pure JSON object which is easier to deal with in modern Web Applications than the XML returned by SOAP.

6.6.4 Process Definition References The MO

Previously the MO has been stored in the UDAs of the Process Definition. Now the Process Definition will only reference the MO. For example, if the MO is a Request, the Process Definition will have a UDA like RequestID. RequestID will contain the unique ID of the Request which typically will be the Primary Key of the Request in the database.

6.6.5 The MO And The Custom Ui

Update the GUI to use these services. Specifically, in addition to the list of Process Instances we now also have a list of the objects we are managing. Eventually, we will make this list sortable and filterable.

MO View when clicking on Work Item: At this point we will have switched the Process Definition over to reference the MO and it will not be embedded in the UDAs. However, we won't yet have the forms created displaying the MO. What do we do in this case? What is the fastest way to get back to a Working App? One way that typically happens is the Data and the Forms are being updated in parallel. I think our diagram actually shows this.

MO History versus the Process History

6.6.6 Manage Object Checklist

❒ You have an ER diagram or other specification that defines exactly the Managed Object exactly.

❒ The MO Repository is deployed and usable.

❒ REST services are implemented and at least for reading and updating the MO.

❒ The Process Definition no longer includes the MO, it references it by its ID.

❒ The Custom User Interface includes a list of Managed Objects that can be sorted and filtered.

6.7 User Interface And Forms

Artifacts

- Activity Documentation (.docx)

- Web forms (.js files)

- Process Definition (XPDL files)

Activities

1. Identify the view for each process activity.

2. Implement forms.

3. Design Process Form.

4. Add reference to the form in the process definition.

This phase deals with adding specific forms in the UI based on the Activity that the user selected from the Work List.

6.7.1 Define Activity Functionality

Go through the activities in the Process Definitions and document what will be displayed to the user at that activity. It may be something as simple as just displaying the generic Activity Form. Or, it may need to be specific with a specific limited set of data from the MO.

Document exactly which parts of the MO can be updated. Also, differentiate between what properties can be updated and what properties must be updated.

6.7.2 Implement Forms

The Form is the custom view of the activity that is shown to the user in the User Interface. Specifically, this is the view of the activity that is shown to the user when they click on the work item in their work list.

In this phase we iteratively add new forms to the solution. The User Interface is now set to check the form on the Activity. If a form is specified, the UI displays that form. Otherwise, it continues to display the generic form.

You should always add the Process Instance ID somewhere on your form (P360?). It doesn't need to be somewhere obvious to the user. This helps administrators and developers quickly find the Process Instance later if there is an issue.

6.7.3 Design Process View

It is often useful to have an overview of the Process. This known as the Process Form. This is a custom view of a Process Instance that is display when the user clicks on the Process Instance in the Process Instance List in the custom UI.

You should always add the Process Instance ID somewhere on your Process form. It doesn't need to be somewhere obvious to the user. This helps administrators and developers quickly find the Process Instance later if there is an issue.

6.7.4 Update Process Definition Forms

In the Process Definition specify the form or forms to display in the Forms list on the properties of the Activity Nodes and the Start Node. The UI reads the Form field in order to know what is should display to user when they click on a Work Item in their work list.

6.7.5 Activity Checklist

❏ Each activity has a defined set of properties documented that can be updated.

❏ Every activity has a form assigned to it.

❏ Each form displays the Process Instance ID somewhere.

6.8 Integration

Artifacts

- Java actions (.java)

- BPM Action GUI Java files (.java)

Activities

1. Identify integration points.

2. Implement BPM actions.

This phase is where we add the integration points to external systems. For example, we may need the system to get a list of products to display in the UI so that we can pick products to add to an order.

6.8.1 Identify Integration Points

Identify points in the process where external systems need to be updated. This may include changes to the MO repository. For example, we probably want the process to be able to update the value of a State attribute on the MO.

6.8.2 Implement Integration

Integration in the process can happen in two directions: incoming and outgoing. Maybe add a chart here with the different types of integration and when they should be used.

Incoming To Bpm

- Java Model API

- Agile Adapter Web Services

- Listeners and Triggers

Outgoing From Bpm

- BPM Actions

- Agents

Incoming Integration

- Introduction to Incoming Integration

- The Java Model API

- Agile Adapter Web Services

- Listeners and Triggers

Outgoing Integration

Integration in Interstage is typically done using either Java or Web Services. Java integration comes in two flavors:

- BPM Actions

- Agents

BPM Actions

A Java Action is a Java class with methods that can be called by a Process Instance. BPM Actions are a Java Actions that also have a User Interface that gets displayed in Interstage Studio.

Typically, a solution uses BPM and Java Actions to implement integration with external systems. For example, the solution could use a Java Action to update the state of a product in a database somewhere.

Developing Actions   Your Java actions should prefix any logging information with the name of the Action and a process instance ID (P360). This is because the Java Action Class runs in the scope of the Interstage Server and there is a lot of other information being put into the server logs. In order to find your Action log entries it helps greatly to have the log entry refer to your action by name. Furthermore, it helps to add the Process Instance ID as typically there are multiple Process Instances executing at any one time.

Invoking Actions   Different Nodes have different Action Sets. Be careful overloading your Process Definition Init Actions. These actions are run synchronously when starting a new Process Instance. Hence, every Action must complete before the report of started returns. So these actions should be fast. However, if there are Actions that if they fail you do not want the Process to start then you put those in the Init. If you have a large number of Actions or long running actions that need to be done at startup, you can include them in an Or Node right after the Start Node.

Agents

Agents have two special features that make them useful:

- They make a choice on an Activity node.

- They can work asynchronously.

Hence, if you need an integration point that must work asynchronously, you will typically want to use an Agent. This includes a situation where you are waiting for an event on some system.

For example, if you are waiting for a specific object to be created in a database you can use the Agent to poll the system. When the Agent doesn't find the object yet, it returns empty string "" to the Interstage Server. Interstage will then invoke the Agent again after a configurable period of time. When the Agent finally finds te object, it returns a string matching the name of the Choice on the Activity node.

As with Actions any logging information that your Agent writes should specifically include the name of the Agent and the Process Instance ID.

6.8.3 Integration Checklist

❐ Add checklist items here.

❐ Your Java Actions include identity and process instance information with any logging information.

❐ Your Agents include identity and process instance information with any logging information.

6.9 Testing

This phase is specifically about testing. However, that doesn't mean that you should only be testing in this final phase. The phase is about testing to verify that the solution is ready for deployment.

6.9.1 Process Migration

Process Migration is a crucial feature that is often overlooked. However, it is important that all Process Instances are able to be migrated. Process Migration can often be used to salvage Process Instances when a bug is found. In order for a Process Instance to be migrated, all of its nodes must have a unique name.

Before deploying to production you should test that Process Instances from every Process Definition can be migrated.

6.9.2 Testing Checklist

❏ You have tested migrating a Process Instance based on every Process Definition.

❏ Add checklist items here.

Chapter 7

Complex Data Options

It is common to need to process a "complex data structure" in a business process. An example of this would be a complicated form, like a tax document. Such a document has many, possibly hundreds of fields, and those field values might be lists of sub-maps of more values. How do you best handle this? There are four different strategies that can be taken, the choice will depend upon the details of how much you want to access the data outside of the process, and how much you want or need the process engine to take care for the data for you. The first couple strategies are the easiest to implement, and they are the most portable, however they will be suitable only up to a certain level of complexity and interoperability. The latter strategies enable applications with very complex and powerful data structure, but naturally this is more effort to implement and manage. For each data structure in an application, you must decide which approach is most appropriate.

7.1 Overview Of The Four Choices

The term "data document" is used below to represent the complex data structure that is needed. It does not need to be a document in a DMS or a file system. It is actually a complex collection of fields. The exact storage for most of the options is the choice of the data architect. But for ease of discussion, we will use the term document.

Strategy 1:	The entire data document is held in the process variables either as a collection of UDAs, as an XML UDA, as a custom data type, or as a UDA holding JSON. The advantage of keeping all the data in the process is that it is easy to set up, no database table needs to be declared, all the data is always consistent with the process definition, and you can use the built in features to track the changes that are made to the data.
Strategy 2:	Data is held in process variables, but synchronized with an external data record. When the data is updated in the process, java actions are called that also update the record in the database. The advantage of this is that standard DB query techniques can be used to find the record, if it is needed regularly outside of the process.
Strategy 3:	Process contains a key for the data record that is kept separately in the database. You can think of this as a data "document" which is attached to the process. The user interface will read the process instance information, and then using the key, read the data from the database. When updating there will be two separate updates as well.
Strategy 4:	The data "document" is primary access point, and the data document contains a key referencing the process (which also probably has a reference key back to the data document). The difference is that in this situation the data document may refer to multiple processes all running representing state of different parts of the document.

In all of these options, the data document is holding a set of data for the case, while the process instance always holds the state of the processing of the document.

7.2 Strategy 1: Fully Contained

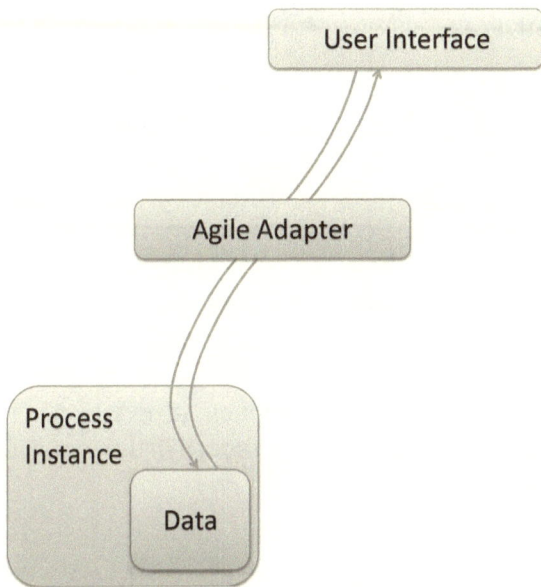

The data is fully contained in the process. This could occupy any number of UDA variables. The data might be simple values, or a record structure composed in XML, JSON, or a customer data type.

When the process is completed, the final data can be written out to an external form for long term records as a final step in the process, but the idea is that during the process execution it is only available through the process.

7.2.1 Advantages

- You don't have to create any table or set up anything to store the data. Just declare the UDA variables in the process definition and everything else is taken care of by the BPM system. Installing an application is easy.

- The data is always consistent with the process state.

- These variables can be marked as worklist UDAs and then are searchable from the worklist and process list.

- They can be marked as tracked, and then the history will keep a record of every time they are changed.

7.2.2 Disadvantages

- You have to access the process instance in order to access the data. You can search process instances, but still you are accessing the process instance and not the raw data. More advanced aspects of finding records, such as joins are not available. This strategy is strongly recommended when putting together any lightweight process where the information is more or less unique to the process. For example, a travel request which is routed through a group of people for approval can be completely contained in the process. There is little reason to refer to a person's travel request outside of the process, at least until it is ultimately approved, and then a permanent record of the result is constructed some place.

7.3 Strategy 2: Synchronized With Database

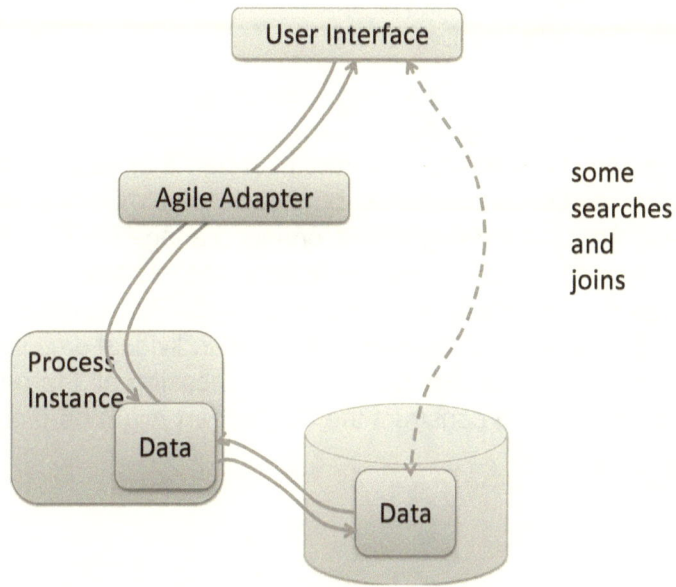

In this case the user interface still uses the Agile Adapter (web service API to the process instance) to read and write the data. The process instance has a copy of the data document. But it also uses DB java actions to reflect the values into an external database at each step of the process. This could be a two way interaction, both reading the data refreshing the internal cache, as well as updating the db when the data is changed.

7.3.1 Advantages

- All the advantages of strategy 1

- The ability to quickly search for cases using external search means.

- If two way update is implemented, then it would be possible to update directly into the database as well.

7.3.2 Disadvantages

- You have to create a table or other data storage, which makes it more difficult to set up the application, install the application, or move a running application.

- Synchronization can be wrong sometimes

This approach is used when for the most part the data is completely controlled by the process instance, but needs to be externally searched and sorted. An example might be a project management system handling lots of small tasks, where you want to at the same time produce charts of all the individual tasks, such as a KanBan chart or a Gantt chart. The processes are still in control of the individual data items representing one line in the Gantt chart, but accessing all the processes every time you need to construct the Gantt chart might be prohibitively slow.

7.4 Strategy 3: External Data Tight Coupling

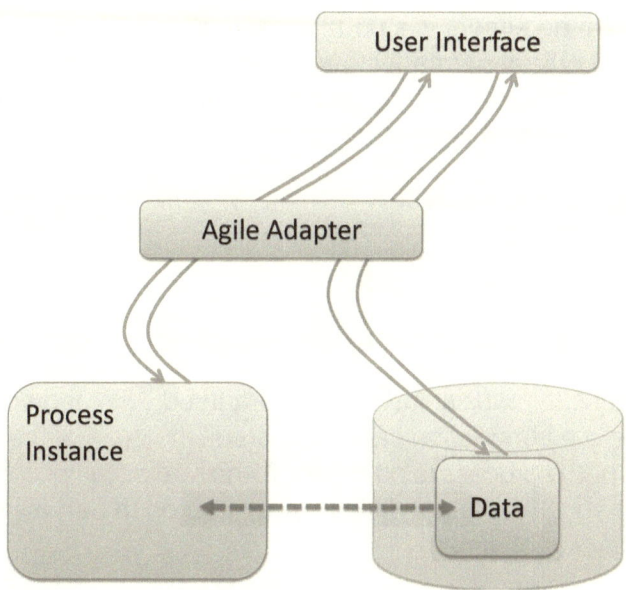

In this approach the data document is kept in a separate storage mechanism, like a database, and it is associated with the process in the same way that an attachment might be. The user interface reads the process information separately from the data document. The process instance holds a key to refer to the data document. Usually the data document will hold a reference to the process (not shown).

The diagram shows using Agile Adapter's data capability, however this could be a completely separate external web service as well.

The data document is then accessible and updatable separately from the process instance. The process instance still holds state of the processing of the data. For example the process may be a complex approval, and the exact state of who has approved, when, and the history of how it got there is still in the process. It is possible for the process to access the data document in order to read values, and it is also possible for the process to update parts of the data document, but for the most part we assume this is rarely needed in this pattern.

7.4.1 Advantages

- Complete Flexibility in how you structure the document.

- If the data document is a permanent record, like a court filing, that forms an official permanent record that must accessible both during processing and after processing, then this pattern gives you the most freedom to do this.

- Allows the use of a data versioning system.

7.4.2 Disadvantages

- You need to set up all the tables or other structures yourself

- Transactional consistent is not guaranteed , instead you need to provide a reconciliation capability to edit the state of the data document or the process to be in sync in the rare occasion that they get out of sync. This is not difficult given that each part is individually consistent at all times.

7.5 Strategy 4: External Data Loose Coupling

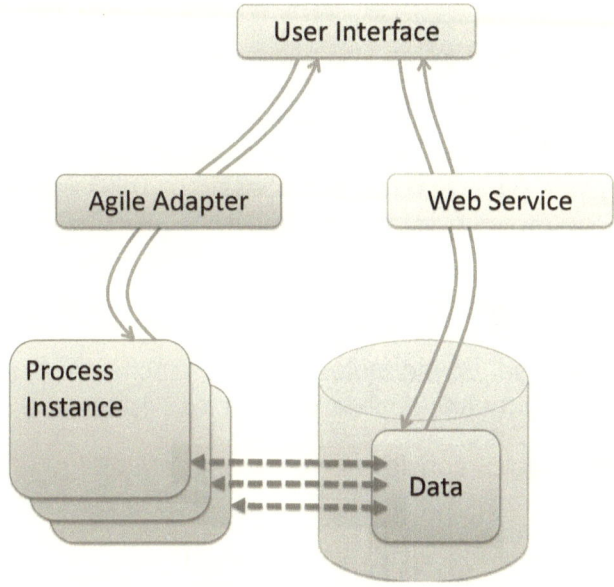

This approach is pretty much the same as the last, but the primary focus is on the data instead of the process. This approach does not require a one-to-one connection between process and data, and this is the preferred approach whenever you need to run a process that refers to part of a data structure. For example, if you have a data document with multiple parts, and each part needs to be approved or processed separately, then you will need a process that is associated with each part of the data document.

The data document (part) refers to the process instance using its global unique identifier. Most of the updating of the data document is directly from the user interface code, through the web service, and this is updated separately from the updates to the process. Each process instance probably also has a reference back to the data so that during process execution it can read or update particular sections of the data.

7.5.1 Advantages

- Complete flexibility in how you structure the data document, versioning.

- This is the most flexible and powerful approach for very complex data requirements.

- The data document can be a permanent record available in the same place during and after processing. This is great for places where the record must be kept forever.

7.5.2 Disadvantages

- You have to set up the tables or other structure manually to store this, and that means applications are less portable.

- No guarantee of consistency between data and process, so this must be address by allowing for manual edits to bring the two back in sync.

7.6 Summary

Four strategies for storing complex data documents with a process are given. The choice should always take as simple and straightforward a strategy as possible that meets the need of the specific application. To be specific, you should take strategy 1, unless you have a good reason to consider a more complicated approach. But if the application requires it, don't hesitate to take the more complicated approach.

All applications will be a mixture of strategies. For example, a hospital admission application might start with a very complex admission form taking strategy 4, but there may be many small processes within the application that use strategy 1. The strategy is based on a data structure basis, determining the approach for that data document, but it does not need to be the same for all data in the application.

Similarly, when taking an external strategy, even within a single process you will find that some of the data will be internal, and some will be external. Sometimes particular data will be duplicated between the internal and external. This is particularly true of data fields that are needed to determine the course of the process, or are needed for properly analysis of the data. For example, even though the hospital administration form is a rich external data document, fields like name, age, and gender are likely to be duplicated as internal data UDA values so that the process can take these into account, and so that analysis can be done on these values.

Most of the flow of data between the data document and the process takes place in the user interface, because that is a place where the data is already being read, and it can simple be stored in both places. There is also the possibility, and it is sometimes necessary, for the process to use Java Actions to read and write from the data document itself.

Between all of these strategies you have a very rich and powerful way to store and manage data for an application.

Chapter 8

Fujitsu DXP Activity Assignment Strategies

BPM processes consist of activities that are done by humans. Who does what activity? A key aspect of the process is determining who should be assigned to an activity. It is not simple, because organizations are always changing; people are leaving, people are joining, people are learning skills, people move to other positions, people take vacations. A proper strategy to assign activities must take into account that the organization will change on a yearly, monthly, weekly, and daily basis and the effort to maintain this must not exceed the value of automating the process in the first place. The most common mistake when first approaching a process model is to assume there is a global group that defines the people who should be assigned to the task. That makes the process easy, but managing a large number of groups, keeping them all up to date, can amount to a large effort, and a critical one since processes go the wrong place if the groups are wrong.

This document will outline all the different techniques that you can use to calculate the people who should be assigned to a particular activity, and so that you can base that calculation on things that are already being maintained.

8.1 Misconceptions

We tend to think of organizations as being static. We see them as things that don't change perceptibly from year to year. "It is the same as it was 5 years ago, and it will be the same 5 years in the future." This is true on some level of abstraction. The mind is amazingly nimble at shifting representations as things change, to represent a new, equivalent representation to use going forward.

An example I often give a VP announcing they are going to retire. This one person, this one change, can have the effect of changing the job of every single person in the organization. The groups that the VP worked directly in will get one person smaller. There are some job functions that will have to be reassigned to other individuals. There may be a person designated to take the place of the VP, but not every job function will be reassigned to this new person who clearly has a different background and somewhat different skills. The leaving of the VP may spell the end of certain initiatives that were particularly promoted by that individual, and will make room for other initiatives by people who remain there. This change in priorities may trickle all the way down to the lowest level groups, causing shifts of people between teams. The very next day, a person in a completely different role is hired, causing another shift in many of the positions on the organization. The next day someone goes home sick, and people need to shift roles to cover urgent tasks that need to be done.

The computer representation of the organization is not abstract. It is very detailed and precise. Software does not deal well with ambiguity. A person is either in a group, or out of a group, but can never be considered to be in a group only when the group really needs it. A person can either have a skill, or not have a skill, but cannot partially have the skill in certain situations. Even the words that we use to describe what people do changes across the organization, across departments, and across regions. A "salesman" for the wealth management service might be an entirely different skill set from a "salesman" for the latest smartphone.

This literal, black-and-white nature of data structures causes harsh difficulties in finding the right person to match with a particular activity. Instead of a binary database on people, you really need a fuzzy knowledge representation of what people do and might be capable of doing, but nobody has such a database today. So we must somehow make it work with an organizational directory that we have today.

8.1.1 Global Groups Are Not Roles

When designing a process, the naïve designer will assign a task to a global group. This will work sometimes. When the group is designed specifically for the application, then it works. For example, in a customer support process, there might be a team in the organizational directory called "support representatives" which is created and maintained specifically so that the support process has tasks for these members. The point is that handing a customer request is such a significant part of the customer support team that defining and maintaining this group properly is essential.

Another area where it can work is when a team is small and the organization relatively small, and the function well defined. An example can be the legal contract review team. If a company of several hundred people has a legal team of 2 or 3 people who are required to review all the contracts, it is reasonable to define a global group with those three names in it and assign a task this way. Another example of this same thing is for special groups of one person, such as CEO, CFO, and other individual roles.

It is easy in these cases to forget that the directory server might not match one-to-one with the organization. For example a company might have a legal entity in Canada, and another in the USA. There would be a CEO for Canada, and a CEO for USA. You cannot count on the CEO identifying one person, nor can you with any other. There might be a Canada legal team, and a UDA legal team. Process designers can mistakenly assume that there is only one, but in fact they need to first identify the organization, and then group within that organization. The group is relative to the organization.

8.1.2 Names Can Be Unspecific

Another problem is when a group represents a job function. For example, a process involving publishing a news article might have a step for an editor, and so assume that there is a group in the organizational directory called "editors". There may be an editors team and appear in the organizational directory, but all editors are not the same. Some editors may specialize in the education market, and others in government publications, and there can be a big difference. Some may be print editors, while others are sound or film editors. If you have a process for managing press releases, the "Editors" group in the corporate directory is probably not appropriate.

Some organizations try to make a group for every application. For example, the process for handling press releases will define a group called "Press Release Editors". Here the problem is that the definition of the set of people is so far away from the application. Someone maintaining the organizational directory would need to be familiar with all the applications that rely on groups defined this way. There can be a lot of those. And when a new person with editing skills joins the company, it is not clear always whether they should be added to the "Press Release Editors" or not – only their manager can say for sure. The implications of adding them are not clear: how many new email notifications will they get? What other things must they be trained in before they are effective? Since this group is specific to the application, it is really better managed together with the application, but putting it in the organizational directory sometimes makes this difficult.

8.1.3 Sticky Roles

When designing a process for writing a book, there will be tasks for the writer to do. In this case, the writer of the book is not just any writer in the organization. If you had an organizational role for "writers", you could not use that for assigning the task, because you need to assign the task to the writer of this particular book. The organizational directory might be useful early on, when attempting to pick a writer for a particular project, but after the process is started you want the same person doing all the writer tasks. The process remembers that person in a structure known as a "role". This is the best thought of as a variable in the process which holds the user id of the person who is playing this role. The role can be changed like any variable, in case you need to reassign the entire project to someone else.

8.1.4 Relationships

Many assignments are required because of relationship. The most common is that of the "manager". We get into more tricky grounds with this. The organization directory often contains a relationship to show the manager that a person reports to, but when you implement business processes, this is not always the manager that is needed. This happens a lot in small offices where a person may be playing the role of several job functions. The receptionist might also be the security person (responsible for the site security) as well as office equipment maintenance. They might report in these various job functions into managers in other parts of the organization. For example, to perform a security function, they might need approval from the corporate security function, and their actual manager might not have anything to do with this.

Like the groups, there often needs to be a special relationship. A good example is a "Medical Emergency Response Team" which are people in the organization who volunteer to be trained to respond in an emergency. If you implement a process, then the organization of these members is completely different than the regular reporting structure. It is possible that a VP level person is serving on the MERT team as a lowest level member, and reports into a person who is otherwise lower rank in the regular organization. You would need to define a special "MERT supervisor" relationship for everyone involved in this function. This is very much like the special groups for specific process applications, and the same warning about the separation of the management of this from the management of the application applies. It might be far better to define and manage this set of relationships in the application itself, but that depends upon the application.

Relationships exist between people, but they also exist indirectly using an organizational unit, or an office location, as an intermediate step. When doing approvals you might need something done by someone who plays a special role in a department. For example, each department might have a finance person who is responsible for managing capital acquisition for that department. One person might be assigned for three departments, but somehow you need to find the right person. You first need to find the department of the requester, and then the right person for that department. This saves you from having to make a unique relationship for every person to the person who manages capital acquisition for them.

8.1.5 Levels

Another very tricky area is that of getting the right number of levels. Imagine a process for approving the shipping of a demo unit (product sample) to a prospective customer. This would normally be done by a salesman, but depending upon the size and value of the product being delivered it might need: (1) their manager, (2) the head of the department, (3) the VP of sales, (4) the CFO, and (5) the CEO. There is a potential for 5 levels of approval needed, on the most expensive cases. But what if the request is made by the head of the department? Does that person's manager need to be involved? What if their manager is the VP of sales, clearly you don't want to count that person twice. It would seem in this case that you only need three people even for the most expensive cases. But there are limits to this. What if the CEO requests it? Even in this case, you still want the CFO and probably the VP of sales involved, because regardless of the status of the person making a request, those people need to be involved.

The rules need to be written in such a way that they naturally get the right answer regardless of the person who makes the initial request.

8.1.6 The Goal

Our goal then is to find a way to

1. determine the best person or group of people to perform a specific task, and

2. do that in a way that imposes only modest effort to maintain.

To do this we need to find a "natural" way to represent relationships, a natural way to express the conditions, so that when an organizational change occurs, a minimal change to the organizational directory will result in

8.2 Strategies

Below are a set of different patterns that you might use to find the right people to assign to activities initially. Different patterns have different implications on the ability to maintain. This list is not exhaustive, but it covers all the most common cases.

8.2.1 1 Assign To Individual Literally

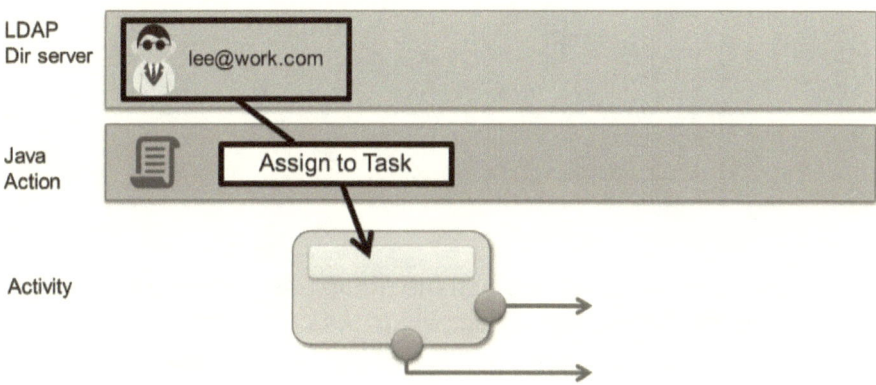

This is the simplest way to assign a particular responsible person to an activity, and it can be used when the designer of the process knows the exact person who will do the activity. In this case, the exact user id of the person who will do the activity is coded directly into the process.

This is accomplished in the Studio by using the "Assign Task To" Java Action in the Role Action Set. This JA has a single input, and you can specify the exact user id as a literal string.

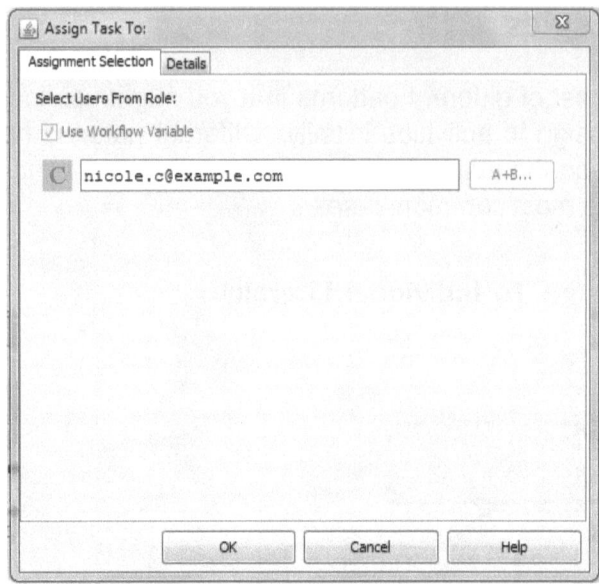

You also need to make sure that the group assignment on the activity is empty so that this does not complicate the calculation.

The problem with this approach is that if you later need to change the person assigned to this task, if someone else is going to step in an do this job for the organization, you need to edit the process definition, and redeploy it to the server. People change jobs all the time, and having to edit the process for each person who changes jobs would be an unacceptable overhead for most organizations. It also makes it difficult to test the process because the administrator of a test server has no ability to reassign things to different people for the purpose of testing. Because of this, the direct literal approach is not recommended for any situation. Instead, make a simple local group, assign the task to that, and allow the administrator to control the actual user who is in that local group.

8.2.2 2. Assign To A Global Group, Not Expanded

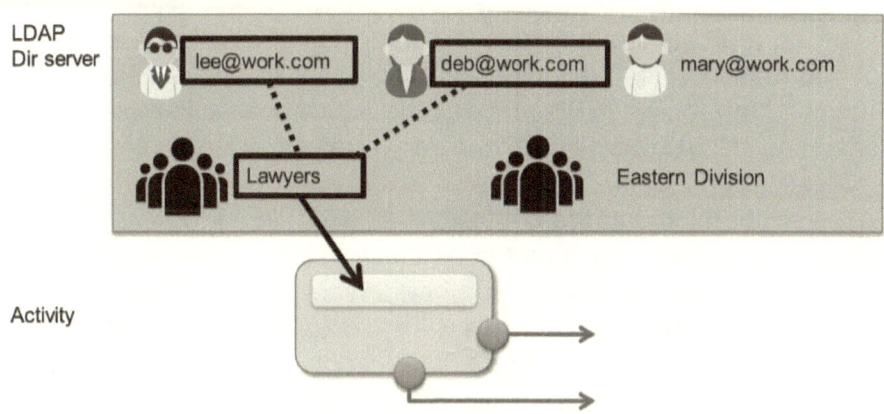

This is the simplest and most direct way to assign an activity, because the activity has a place to specify the "Assignee". Just enter the name of the group in this space, and you are done.

In this example the name "Lawyers" would contain a person, or a list of people, who have been designated by the organization to perform legal duties. Any task that must be done by a lawyer, such as contract review, can be assigned to this group. At the time we design the process, we don't need to know specifically who this is. We only need to know the name of the group. At runtime, the server will look up the group, and assign the task to the members of the group.

Assignee

Group: Lawyers

☑ Expand Groups

The group that you specify here can exist either in the list of global groups that is retrieved from the LDAP server, or it can be the name of a local group that is specified in the BPM server tenant space. If the group is defined in the LDAP directory, then the members of the group can be specified only by a person who has administrative access to the LDAP directory server, which can be a good thing if the group in question is quite well known and used in multiple applications. Requiring and enforcing a global group across the organization tend to be a problem for two reasons. (1) While fine for production, testing is complicated. Running the process really requires the actual production users, even for testing. (2) A global group can very rarely be used across multiple applications.

You might think that the company has a single set of lawyers, until you look at the processes that need these users. Some lawyers might be there to review contracts, but other lawyers could be there for many other purposes, such as patent law, intellectual property management, or even criminal law. You might have people who just happen to be lawyers, such as the CEO, who is not operating actively in that capacity. What does the group "lawyers" really mean? Does it mean anyone with a law degree? Does it mean people who have passed the bar exam? Do they have to be active lawyers, or would you include anyone who had been a lawyer at one point in time? Does it mean that these people are available for any legal task in the organization? When you start looking at the tasks that lawyers do, you find that there are many kinds of lawyers, who do different things. Do you include legal assistants in the group, because often you will find there are tasks for the lawyer to do, but they have empowered their assistant to do these tasks for them; you would assign a task to the assistant, and not the lawyer. Who you include in a group called "lawyer" depends very much on how you expect to use that group, and it is not clear from the name how you will use it.

Assignee

Group: ContractReviewers

☑ Expand Groups

It is a good practice then to define groups by names that clearly state what the group will be used for, which in practice means what tasks will be assigned to the group. For example, you might define a group named "ContractReviewers" to make it clear that they people in this group should all expect to be assigned tasks to review contracts at some time.

This may seem clear, but it still can be problematic. There may be some people in the organization qualified to review sales contracts, but other lawyers are needed to review real estate contracts. The subtle difference between groups is not spelled out in the name, and using that same name on a variety of different activities is unlikely to work. What we find in practice is that within a single application, you will need to define groups that are related to specific sets of activities. Thus a sales process will define a group, and the meaning of that group is unique to the sales process.

Local groups are more suitable for most applications. The application requires a group with a particular name to run, but actually the group is defined in the tenant. Each tenant can specify the users who are members of a particular group. If you have multiple applications installed into a tenant, they must use the same definition for a particular group. This is usually not a problem if you make a modest attempt to give groups names that are specific to the application, and avoid extremely generic names like "workers" which might apply to anyone.

8.2.3 3. Assign To Global Group, Expanded

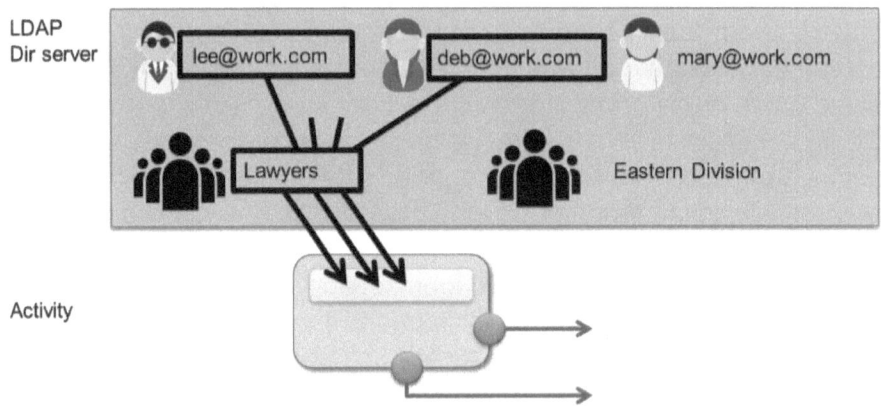

If you have "Expand Groups" checked, then the server will look up the members of the group at the time that the activity is started, and assign the group to every member of the group. If the group has 5 people, then 5 work items will be created, one assigned to each group member. It goes into a queue for the individual user, and every work item for that user, no matter which process no matter which application goes into the same inbox.

This allows for a pull style assignment. One of those people might accept the task, which reserves the task to them, and effectively pulls the task away from the other members of the group.

When a group is not expanded at the time that the activity starts, then

- A single work item is created for the group as a whole

- A user must specify the name of the group when requesting work items.

- Users joining a group later will have access to uncompleted work items.

- Users who leave the group will be immediately cut off from the work item

The difference is simply that group membership counts at the time that you get the work item, instead of at the time that the activity is started.

This makes a difference for activities that might last a long time, and for which the members of groups might change over the time the activity is active.

Applications that use this approach has a slightly different feel to them. The user would retrieve the work items assigned to "ContractReviewers" instead of just getting all work items assigned to them. That list would have all the tasks for contract reviewers to do, but none of the tasks of any other role that the user might be playing. Instead of a single inbox with all the tasks in it, the user tends to specify a particular kind of role first, and then find the work items available for that role. The user might need to check several task lists to see what is pending for them. In some applications this is acceptable, particularly when a user is involved in an application only for a single kind of task.

8.2.4 4. Assign To Local Group, Not Expanded

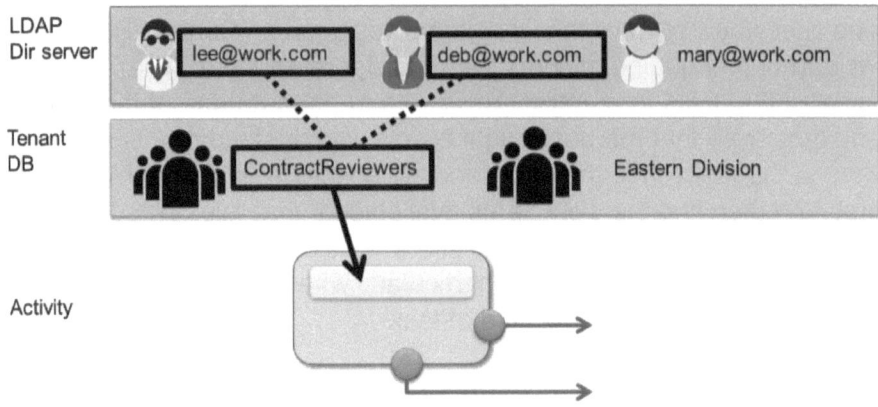

As mentioned above, in reality most group will be specific to the particular application, to the particular set of activities that are all being done. Because of this it can be more convenient to manage that group as part of the application, and not the LDAP directory. Fujitsu DXP has a way to define groups directly in the server (the tenant, to be specific). The members of this group can be managed by the application itself.

When assigning non-expanded, the task is assigned to the group as a whole, and the user has to ask for all the work items assigned to that group.

8.2.5 5. Assign To Local Group, Expanded

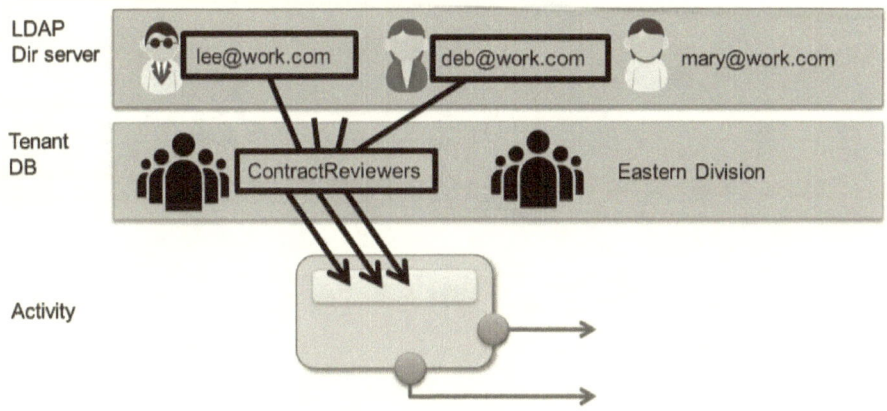

Like the global group, you can decide to expand the group to member users at the time that the activity is started, or not. Each user will receive a work item addresses directly to them, and no matter how many applications they are involved in, all of the work items can be listed in a single inbox.

8.2.6 6. Assign To Previous Actor

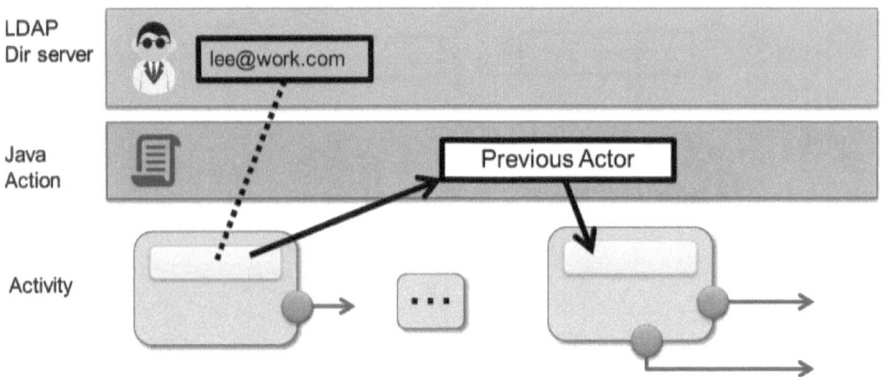

It will often be the case that a process will need the same person to do two different actions at different times. A good example is a request application, where one person makes a request. Commonly, there will be other things for the requester to do.

Fujitsu DXP has a specific capability to assign one activity to whoever completed an earlier activity. You create a "Previous Actor" java action in the Role action set.

You select the name of the other activity in the activity name prompt. The pulldown list will include all of the activities in the process.

At run time, the server will look and find out who performed that earlier activity, and will assign this activity to the same user. This is straightforward and useful, but has only one drawback: when a significant amount of time has passed, it may be that the organization has changed during that time.

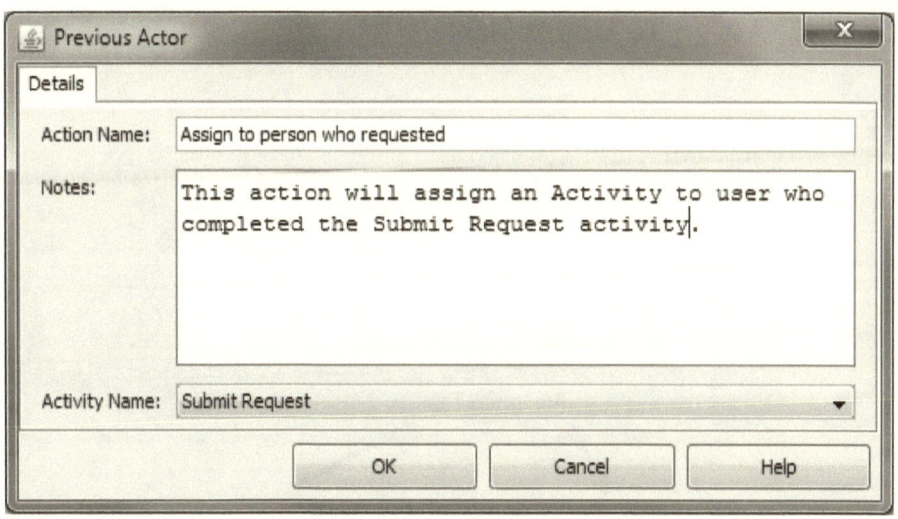

One person might request a purchase of something that the department needs. But then people are moved around, reassigned to different jobs, possible to different departments. A different person has become responsible for the purchase, but there is no way for the process to know that. It will assign tasks to the original person. Fujitsu DXP gives you the ability to reassign tasks after the activity is started, and that is one way to address the situation, but be aware of the effect that an organizational change might have on your processes.

8.2.7 7. Assign To Uda Variable

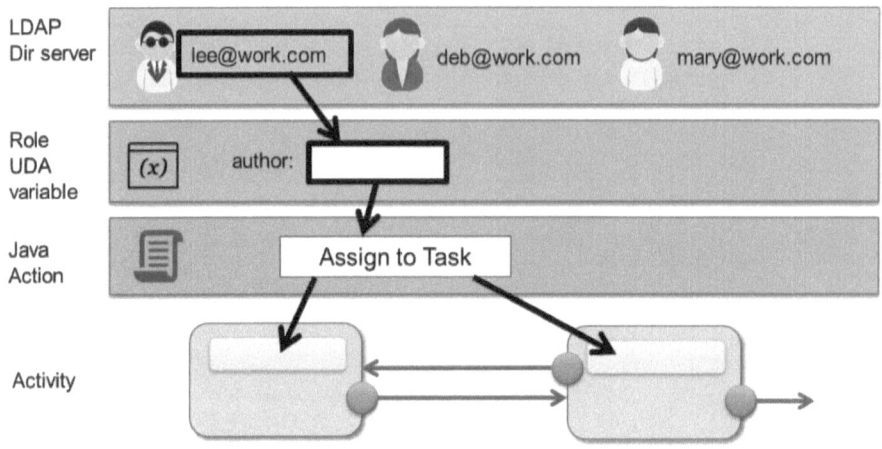

This is the most powerful technique used by most applications. You create a UDA variable in the process for the role that is being performed. The variable is set to the user who is designated to perform a set of activities for that process instance. For example, consider the process to prepare an article for publication in a newspaper. That article will have an author. You would create a UDA variable called "author". This variable would be set early in the process, and all activities that need to be done by the author will be assigned by the user specified by the variable.

This approach is powerful because:

- Each instance of the process can be assigned to different people.

- The variable can be changed in the middle.

The role player is specific to the process instance. This allows the process itself to manage the people who play the various roles on a case by case basis. It is a more natural way of thinking about a role in a particular process. Some logic can be used to identify the best person early on, and then all the activities are assigned consistently. For some processes, it does not matter who gets assigned initially, but it is important that further activities keep getting consistently assigned to the same person. For example, a customer support case: the person who initially picks up the case could be arbitrary, but after the handling of the case is started, it is useful to keep the same person involved.

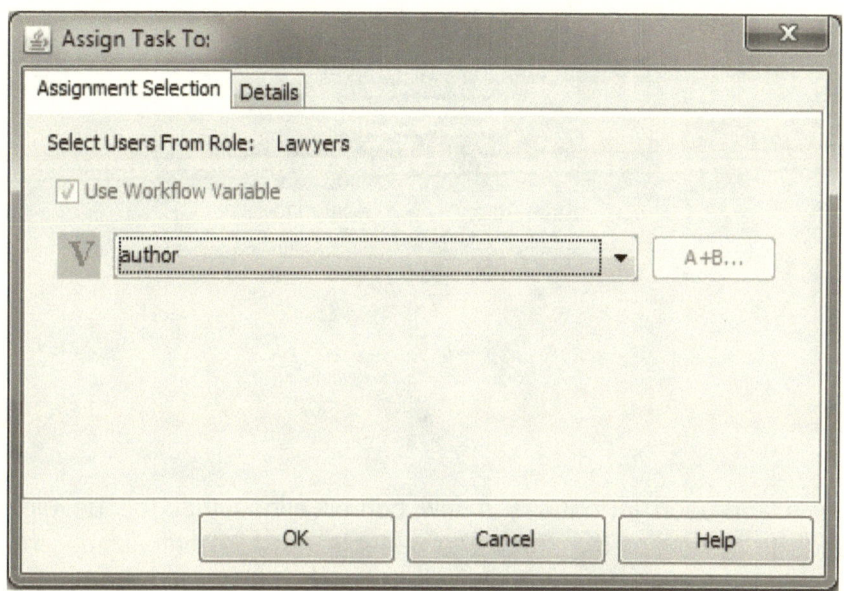

The role player can change, and that change "sticks". For example, the half-completed newspaper article could be assigned to a different person who then is assigned to the remaining activities. Assigning and reassigning individual activities is sufficient when a person interacts only with a single activity in a process. But if a person is to do multiple, and you want the ability to reassign the entire process, then you need a variable to hold this.

8.2.8 8. Initializing Variable From Earlier Action

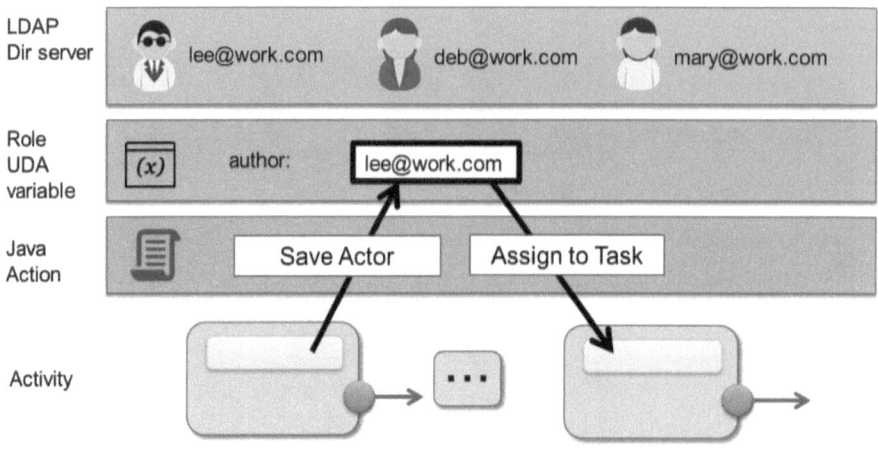

This approach introduces a few complications that the developer needs to be aware of. First, the variable must be initialized. If the variable is empty when an activity that needs it is started there can be problems. There is a java action that is particularly convenient for initializing the variable, and that is to capture the user name of the person who does a particular activity early in the process. For example, you might assign the first activity in a customer support process to a group of support people. One person might take that case, and complete the first activity. The epilogue action set would then include this java action to save the user id of the person who did that:

This action is on an activity, and when that activity is completed, the UDa variable (author) will be initialized to whoever completed the activity. Later activities use this variable, and the result is that later activities will be assigned to whoever completed this activity. It is just like the "Previous Actor" example with one important difference: since a variable is involved, you can display this person, and you can change it if necessary.

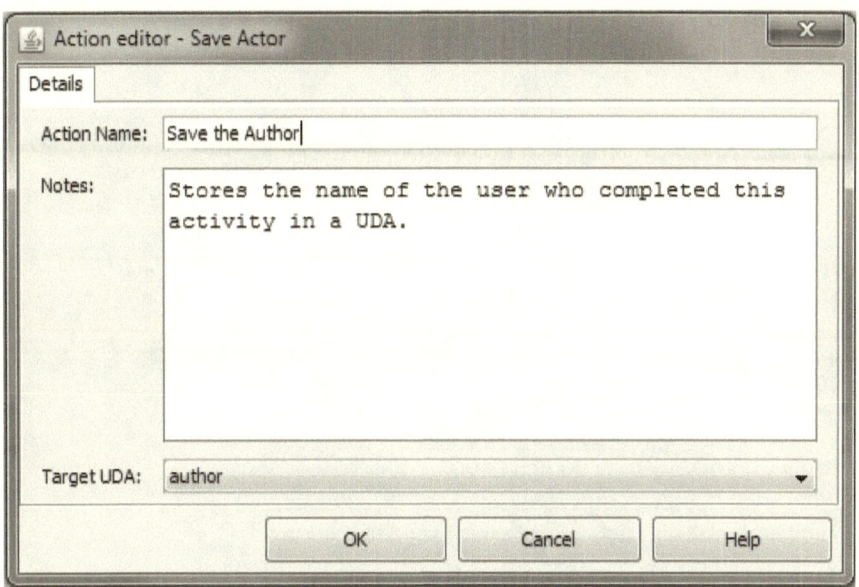

If you have a process where the same person needs to do more than one thing, use this approach. Also, if you have a process where one person decides who will do a particular job, use this approach as well, since a variable could be assigned through the user interface.

8.2.9 9. Uda Variables With Lists

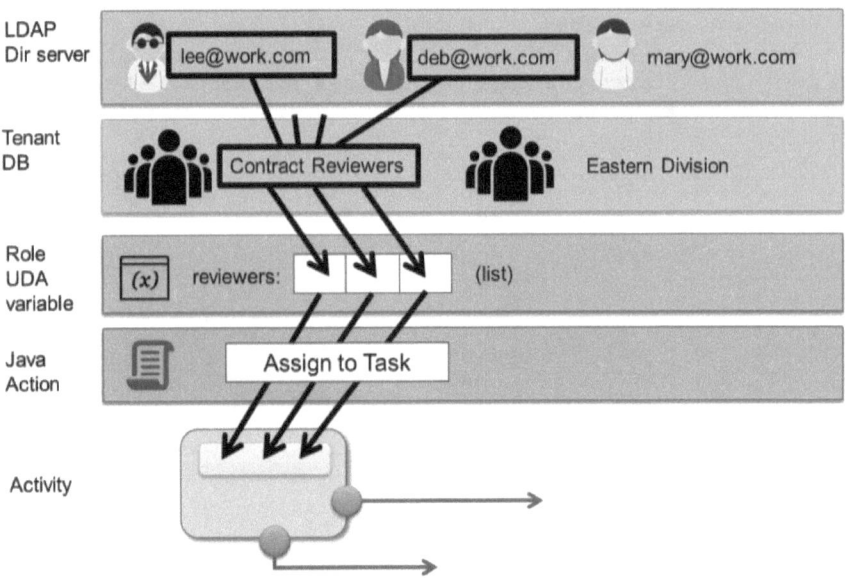

Another powerful technique is to use the UDA variable to store a list of user names. Each name in the list is separated by commas. This is essentially the same as the previous option, with the only difference being that instead of one person playing the role, you have a list of people playing the role. Presumably, it does not matter which one takes each activity, only that someone in that list does.

There are java actions that help support lists. The process can start by reading all the members of a group. This is done by a java action called either "Get Group Members" or "Get Role Members" (it depends on the version of the product, but the java actions does the same thing.) In this java action you specify the name of a group (either a global group in the LDAP directory, or a local group set in the tenant). You specify the UDA variable to put the group members into, and those members will be put in there as a list with commas between the member names. In this example, you might read a group named "AllWriters" which would include all the writers in a particular organizations, and place that list of writers into the author UDA variable for this process. Presumably, further manipulation of the variable might further isolate who becomes the author for this particular article.

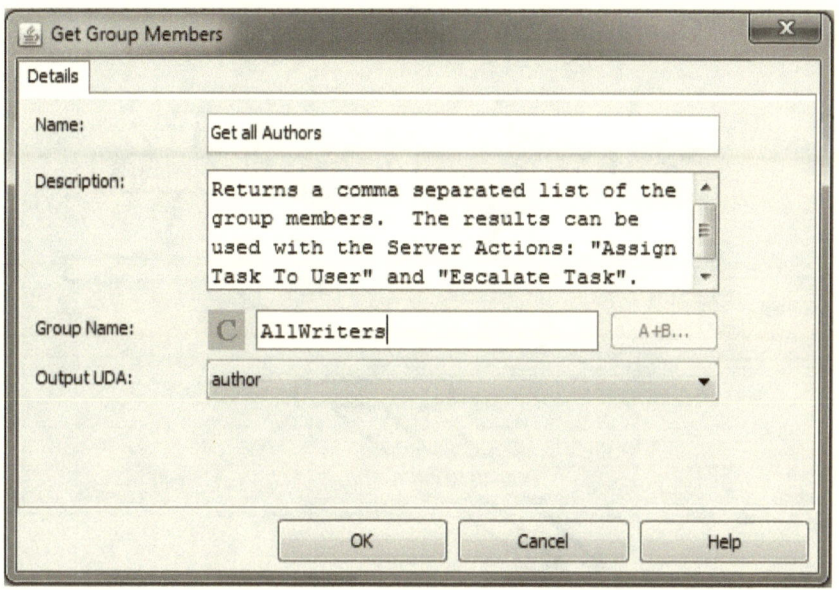

8.2.10 10. Operations On Groups

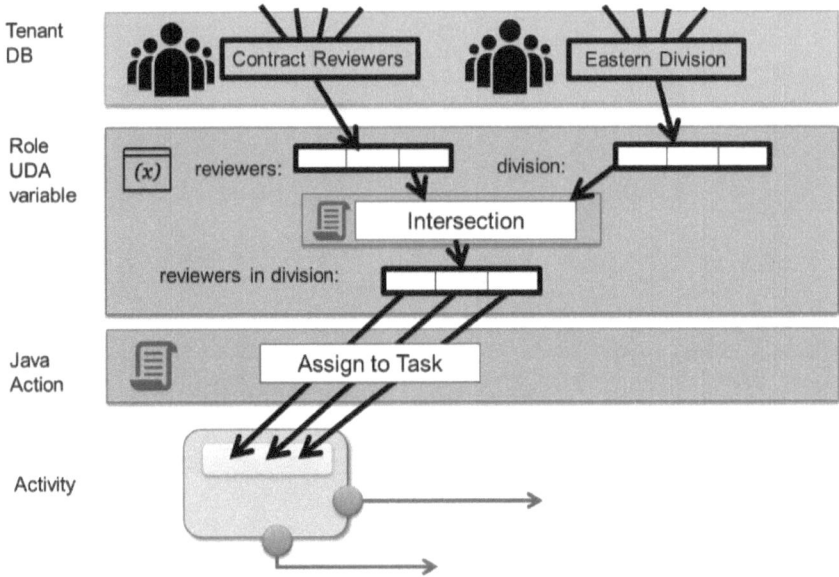

Once you have the ability to read groups of users you can combine groups in various ways. The reason to do this is to define in the directory simpler groups, and then use the group operations (actually the list operations) to derive the more detailed list of people to assign to.

You can find the intersection of two groups. Say you had a group for all a people who are writers in the company. Say you had a second group with all the people at a particular division or location. You could use the intersection command to find all the writers in a particular division, or at a particular location.

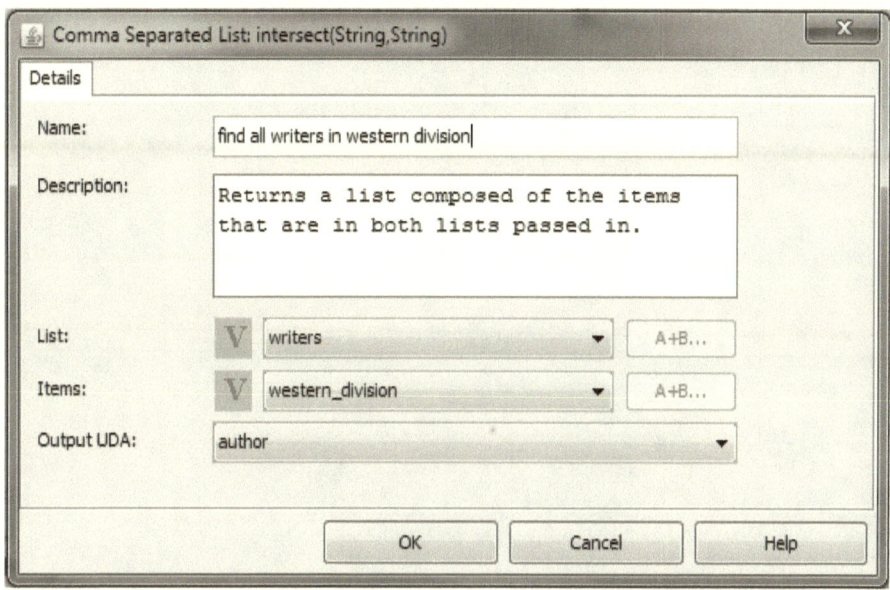

You can combine two groups together using the union command. This combines the lists, but it eliminates duplicates. Say you calculated all the writers in the western division and all the writers in the eastern division, you could combine them together and have a list of all the writers from east and west, but excluding all the other writers in the organization.

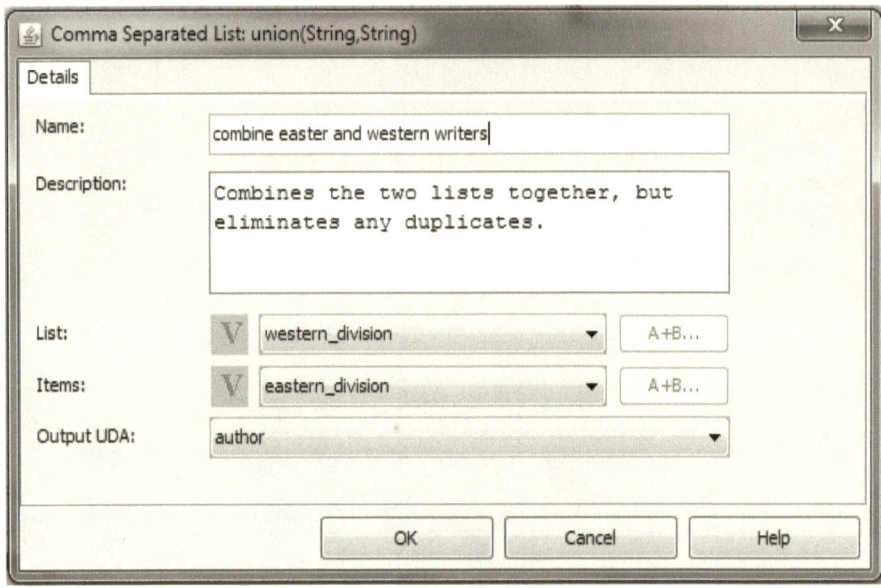

If you have a list, you can remove the members that appear in another list. For example, you might have the all the writers in the western division, but you need to exclude people who are in another list for part-time people. By excluding the part time people, you will be left with all the writers who are full time or other designation if there is any.

8.2.11 11. Direct User Input

We have discussed how UDA variables can contain the name of a user, or a list of users. We call that variable a role because it specifies a particular relationship between those users and the process, and because a set of activities will be assigned to that list of users.

It is worth pointing out that a common way to specify the users that fill those roles is to have the user specify this directly in the user interface. Thus a writer of a book, might specify the editor and the graphic artists to be included in the process as well. The advantage of this is that the person specifying might apply any amount of specialized rules (such as relating the importance of the book with the value of the resource, estimates of who might be most available, and conversations with others about who might be allowed) and incorporate that before choosing a person and putting them into the role. Case management approaches tend to prefer this direct assignment approach.

8.2.12 12. Decision Tables Generate A List

Like the other ways to generate a list, you can leverage a decision table to have complex rules around who must be involved in a particular role.

8.2.13 13. Accumulated List

Another fairly common approach is to collect a list of users as the process moves forward, for some actions later in the process. For example, the process may start by working through a list of of people. Each person assigns to the next. For example, person A chooses person B. Then person B chooses person C, and so on. As each person gets chosen, they are placed on the end of a list UDA. This results in a complete list of everyone who had been involved. Later in the process, you might use that list to do another action, such as an approval action, that involves all the people who were involved in assigning the activity in the first place. There is a java action to reverse the order of the list in case you want to get those approvals in the opposite order that they were placed in there. Another common use for this is in an approval loop: when each person approves you include that user id into a list. IF anyone in the list rejects the proposal, then you can email all the people who have approved before, and let them know that it was rejected. It is important to let people know who had been involved before, but leave out people who had not been involved before.

8.2.14 14. Assign To First In List

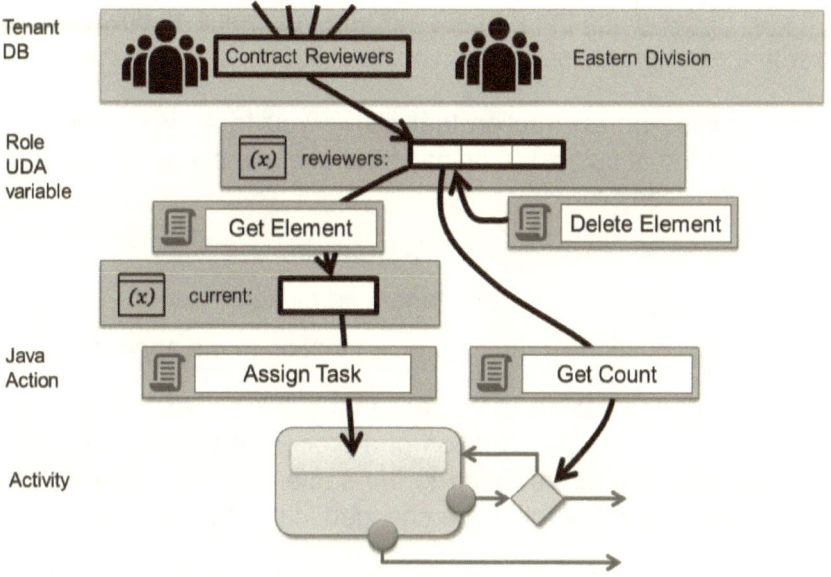

Given that you have a list of people to do a task, you may not want to give it to them all at the same time. The standard approval process has one person at a time approving. The reason for this is to reduce the load on the people at the higher levels until after those at the lower level have approved. Given that you can calculate the list of people who need to be involved, and given that list is sorted in the order that you want to see assigned to activities, you can pull users one at a time and assign the activity to them one at a time.

There is a java action to select a particular element from the list. You would choose element number 0 to get the first in the list and put it in another UDA. You then remove element 0 from the list. Finally, you assign the activity to that user you placed in the new UDA.

You can loop back if the list has one or more users remaining. There is a java action that returns the number of elements that remain in the list, and you make the loop by testing the length of the list, and looping back when there are still elements in the list.

8.3 Summary

Determining who is going to be assigned (initially) to a task is an important part of designing the process. Where you boil it all down, you end up with these primary elements:

- **Groups:** an abstraction that allows you to assign a name to a collection of users, but manage the users in the group separately. Groups can be

    - global – managed by LDAP admin,
    - tenant – managed by tenant admin, or
    - application – managed by a function of the application

- **Role Variables:** an abstraction that holds a particular user or list of users across the duration of a process instance. Subsequent activities can be assigned to the same, and also allowing those designated in the role to be changed in the middle of the process.

- **Initial players:** There are various ways to take in the group members to role variables and combine, intersect, exclude, and dynamically update so that you end up with a reasonable starting assignment.

- Methods of Assignment: offers a few options as well:

    - unexpanded group – gives you a worklist for the group always current
    - expand assign all – at the time of start assigns to everyone in list
    - expand assign individually – pick users one at a time

The various strategies for assigning an activity fall out of combinations of these.

There is one more thing to keep in mind: these strategies are about assigning an activity at the time that it starts. Once the activity is started, it is possible to reassign the work item to other people. In some ways this reduces the risk of assigning beforehand. If it is determined to be assigned to the wrong person, that can be corrected. This is very important for a manager trying t balance work on the team. No matter how careful you try to distribute work, different work is different and may pile

up, and a manager can reassign work to different people. You do, however want to get as close as possible to the optimal person from the start,
and Fujitsu DXP gives you many powerful ways to do this.

Chapter 9

Javascript User Interfaces For Process Driven Solutions

This document discusses some of the merits of using a Web Application built using HTML, JavaScript, and CSS to create custom user interfaces for Process Driven Solutions based on Fujitsu DXP.

As customers are familiar withASP.NET, some comparisons to ASP.NET are made in this document to highlight features and benefits of JavaScript

9.1 Javascript Frameworks

There are many excellent JavaScript frameworks available. This document will discuss AngularJS as it is currently one of the most mature and popular JavaScript Frameworks. However, most of these discussion points would also apply equally as well to React which is the other major player.

9.2 Technical Benefits Of Javascript

This section discusses some of the technical merits of using a Web Application built using HTML, JavaScript, and CSS to create custom user interfaces for Process Driven Solutions based on Fujitsu DXP.

Specifically we discuss areas of:

- Platform Support

- Rich User Experience

- Separation of Declarative and Functional Code

9.2.1 Platform Support

JavaScript runs in the browser. Hence, pages with JavaScript can be served from any Web server technology. When using HTML with a JavaScript Framework your Web Application is able to run on the same Web platform as the Interstage Server. Often this platform will be JBoss.

As a comparison ASP.NET is only supported by IIS. Hence, you specifically need to deploy your Web Client on a separate server from the Interstage server.

9.2.2 Rich User Experience

Modern Web Development using JavaScript can create a rich user experience that previously was only available in Windows based fat clients. Two examples of this are:

- Responsive

- Real Time

Responsive

A responsive Web UI changes its layout based on the screen configuration. For example in a browser on a smart phone the UI changes to be narrower and more vertically arranged.

By leveraging Bootstrap, JavaScript applications can easily provide a responsive UI. While it is true that Bootstrap can also be leveraged by ASP.NET applications, some of Bootstrap is based on JavaScript. Hence, using it in ASP.NET implies a mixing of JavaScript and ASP.NET.

Real Time

Even though the interface is Web Based users expect sections of the screen to update without having to do a page refresh. AngularJS makes this easy to implement with its two way binding without extra effort.

9.2.3 Separation Of Declarative And Functional Code

HTML is Declarative while JavaScript is Functional. A JavaScript Web application specifies the content or Presentation in HTML files. And JavaScript files specify the functionality.

One of the main challenges of ASP.NET is that it embeds server code in the HTML pages. This mixing of presentation code (View), and functional code (View Controller) and even processing code impacts development in many areas such as:

- Maintenance

- Testing

- Multiple Contributors

Maintenance

Since the presentation layer is embedded in the server code, it makes the code more difficult to follow, especially for developers new to the project trying to learn the code.

Debugging the code is difficult as you need to first detect which layer is the root cause of any issue.

These Makes the code more difficult to maintain.

Testing

In order to test ASP.NET your server code must be working. HTML and JavaScript are easy to quickly run and test. Test early, test often!

Multiple Contributors

The mixed code, especially in large environments like RQ, makes it difficult to separate duties among contributors. In a JavaScript environment, especially when using a framework like Angular, there is a clear separation between what is on the server side and what is purely presentation layer processing

The presentation layer is written in a Declarative style in pure HTML and the functional code is written in separate JavaScript files. Again, this provides an even clearer separation of duties. This also lets graphical designers focus on the design aspects of the interface without being distracted by the embedded server code.

9.3 Logistical Reasons

Even if we ignore the technical factors there are two good logistical reasons to use JavaScript for UI development. That is:

- Reusable Components

- JavaScript Form Training

9.3.1 Reusable Components

Fujitsu provides reusable BPM components built in AngularJS. These components can be leveraged to quickly create customized user interfaces that display things like task lists, process lists, etc. Also, there are controls for actions such as making a choice, reassigning, suspending, etc.

9.3.2 Javascript Form Training

Fujitsu has in depth experience in creating JavaScript solutions based on Interstage. Furthermore, Fujitsu is providing training to customers in creating forms using JavaScript.

Chapter 10

Web Service Documentation Requirements

This document serves explores what is required from a web service provider in order to consume that web service using Fujitsu DXP.

This document is preliminary and will be revised after the first couple of BPM projects are completed to take into account specific recommendations learned while implementing these projects.

10.1 Web Service Assumptions

A web service include any kind of network deployed resource for which a structure message can be sent, and a structure response message is returned.

Most web services are synchronous, which means that a TCP/IP connection is set up, the request is made, and the response is returned before the connection is broken. Some web services are asynchronous such that a connection is made and the request sent. Then the connection is dropped, and the response is returned another way.

Most web services will be a SOAP style web service, which has an interface that is defined by a WSDL file. Structured data is sent most often encoded in XML, defined by an XML Schema, often embedded in the WSDL document.

ReST style web services are assumed to be less common at this point, and would need to have detailed documentation. These web services may use JSON instead.

10.2 Required Information

10.2.1 Transport Level

The WSDL file dines most of the parameters needed to set up a call. It is imperative that these are specified clearly and correctly:

- service - defines the overall service which is a collection of operations.

- binding – this gives critical details on how to connect to and request the operations. Only http bindings will be supported.

- port type – defines the inputs and output for a particular operation

- message definitions – provide the details for the input and output messages. The messages might leverage data structures defined in the types section.

- types – this is where all of the schema definitions for the messages must be defined. All schemas should be included in the WSDL file so that it is a complete package usable without retrieving any external reference.

The schema defines the form of the data structure to a fairly good detail. For the leaves of the tree it defines the primitive data types (strings, int, long, date) and can also define constraints such as minimum values, maximum values, patterns that must be matched, as well as lists of values that are allowed.

10.2.2 Information Level

While the schema gives the form of the data structure, it can not express very much about the meaning of each of the data values. It is necessary then to have a complete document that describes all of the leaf data values completely.

Official Name

The official name will uniquely distinguish this service from all the others.

Version Level

The service may have been deployed earlier in different versions fo the service. the documentation must clearly state the version that this doc-umentation is referring to, and the dates that that service was (or will be) put into service.

High Level Description

There must be a complete high level description of what the service does. This should include a conceptual description of the information that it will accept in, and the conceptual description of the information that will be returned.

Detailed Data Field Descriptions

The leaf values are the ends of the trees and that is where the data structure has basic data values included. These will be integers, string, dates, floats, etc. The meaning and relevance of the value must be clarified. If this is an input structure then is should document what the effect of different values would be.

This is probably the longest and most important part. There must be enough information provided for the caller to know how to transform data that is in the process into the correct form for making the request. It also must describe the returned data in enough data to know how to parse the relevate values out that are useful to the process.

Some fields allow multiple values, and the minimum and maximum number of values that are allowed should be clearly specified. Maximum size of data fields allowed should be specified as well so that the caller can truncate the data in the request, or at the very least be prepared that the response will be subject to truncation.

Error Responses

If the web service will return an error when a nonsense request is made, then the form of that error response must be specified so that the process can handle it appropriately.

Failure Responses

To be distinguished from the errors (which were well formed request with data that does not make sense) the failure response is how the supporting infrastructure handles requests that are not valid.

Performance Level Agreement

How long does it take to make a single request and get a response. How many requests can be made in a unit of time.

Authentication Considerations

In the Revenu Quebec environment, many server run as a particular identity, and this identity is communicated to the web service. This allows the access to be controlled strictly from server to server. Any special requirements about the identity of the service making the call should be specified in the documentation.

Security Considerations

What requirements exist around the what the process must have in order to make a call to the server. For instance, if the service is providing information that should only be given to a process that is handling a particular citizen account, then the process may be required to verify that it is to some degree of certainty handling a request from that citizen before making the request. This might or might not be enforced, and if it is not enforced, then the requirement must be clearly stated in documentation.

Privacy Considerations

If the information being returned is sensitive and must be handled ina specifi way, then those handling requirements must be part of the documentation for the web service. The calling application must either provide the appropriate level of data isolation and data protection that conforms to this condition, or it must not make the call.

Responsible Parties

The documentation must include the name of at least one person who is responsible for the development of the service and can support the usage of that service. It also must include the name of an escalation party who is prepared to respond to run-time problems with the execution of the service. These will need to be listed in a place that can be updated frequently, and referred to readily in case there is an emergency.

Future Directions

No service is entirely static, and if there are intents to provide either expanded or diminished service in the future, or to recommend that people us a migration path to another service, this should be documented along with any anticipated time line.

10.3 Usage In Fujitsu DXP

Below is an example of how web services are set up in Fujitsu DXP intended as a resource for readers to understand why certain things might be required of the web service.

In Fujitsu DXP, everything starts with a WSDL file. in the first screen of the web service action, you enter the path to the WSDL file, along with a name and description of what this action is doing at this point in the process.

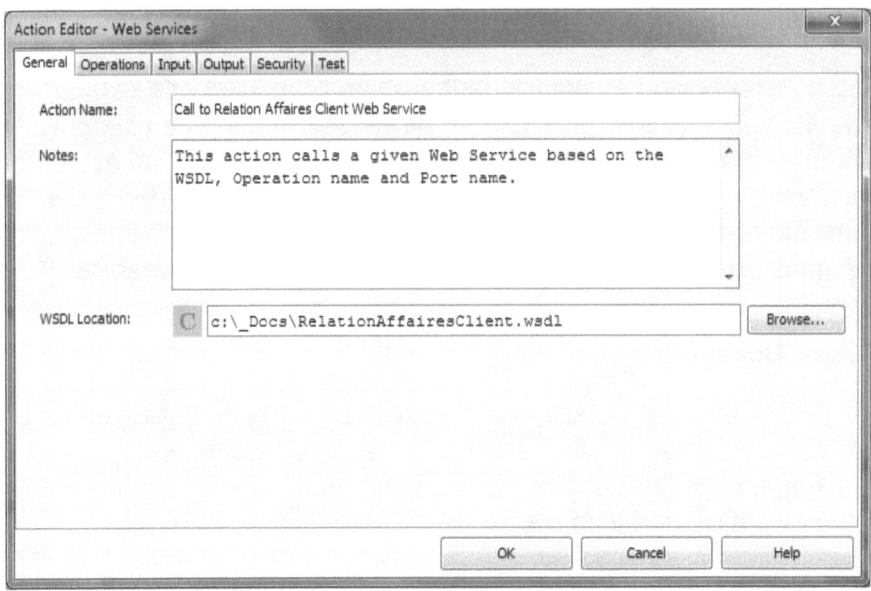

The first press of the "OK" button saves these values, and reads the WSDL file, which provides the metadata for filling in the rest of the panes.

Then clicking on the Operations tab, you have a panel that allows the process designer to select the service, the port, and the operations that you want to call. This may be saved in a UDA variable for further usage.

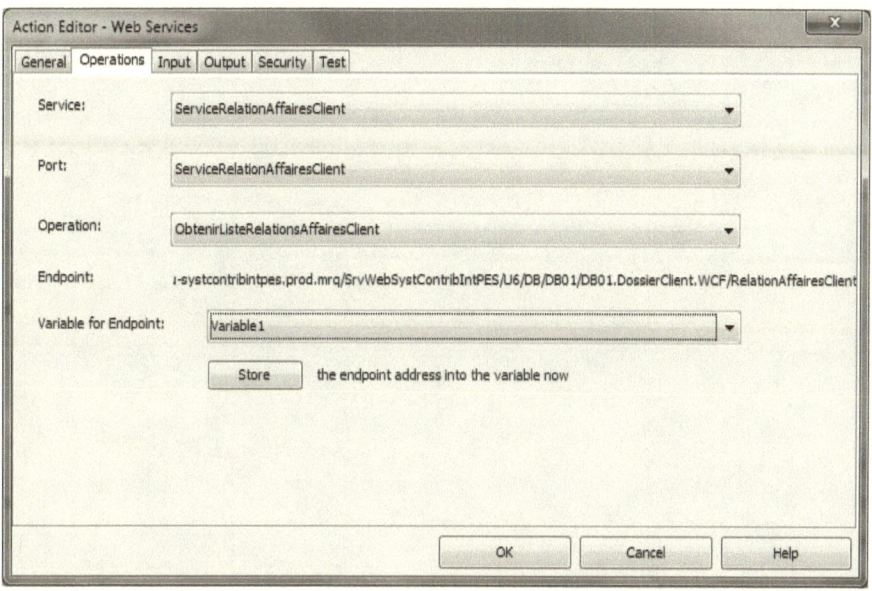

The input tab uses the schema speficied by the WSDL to construct an XML input message. The box allows the designer to specify UDA values that are then placed into the structure at locations specified by the XPath expressions. Any number of values from UDAs can be inserted into the structure. Editing the XML directly allows placing constant values in the structure as well.

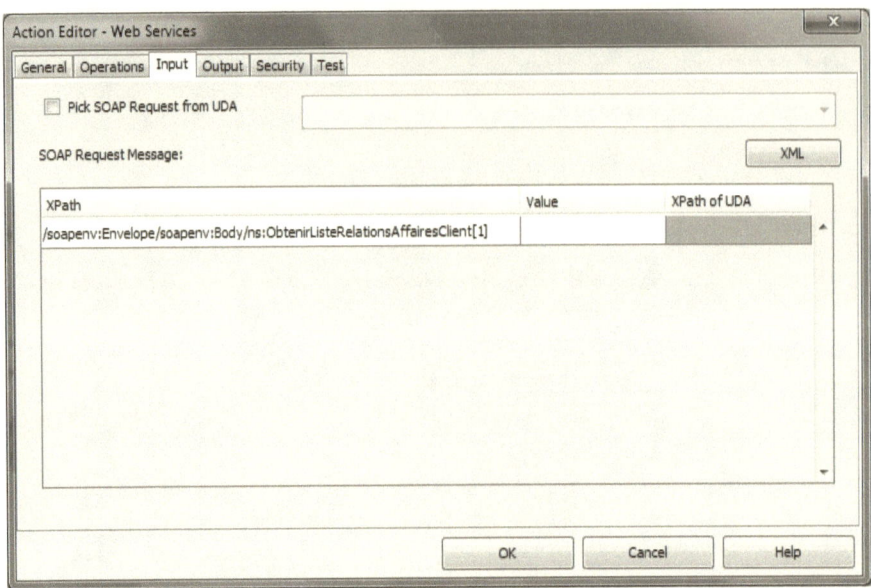

In the above example there was only a single element in the WSDL schema, but normally there would be a more elaborate XML structure.

The output tab then displays the XML structure from the schema in the WSDL file. Again, XPath expressions can be used to take values from the middle of the XML and place them into UDA variables. Supporting the user with all the possible path expressions is why it is so important that the schema be complete in the WSDL files.

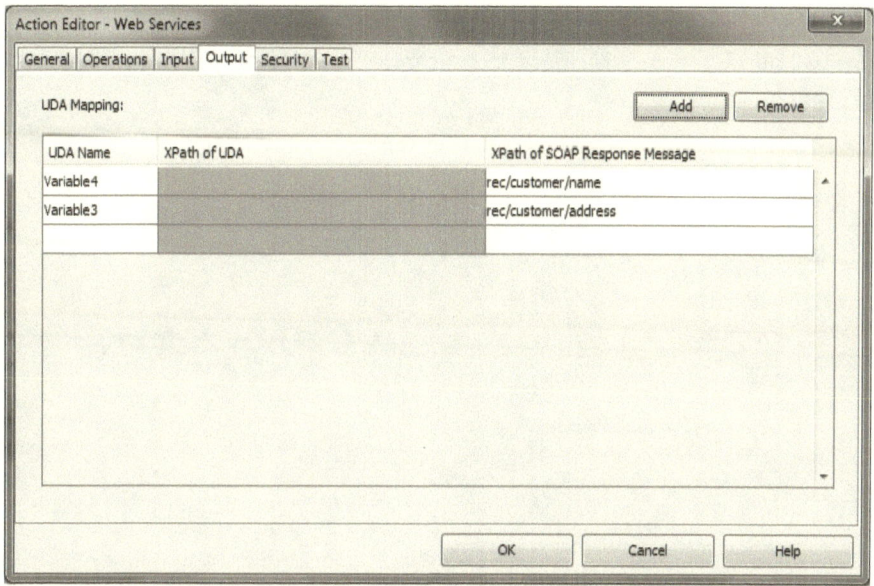

The security tab allows the user to specify the user and ppassword for basic authentication to the web service.

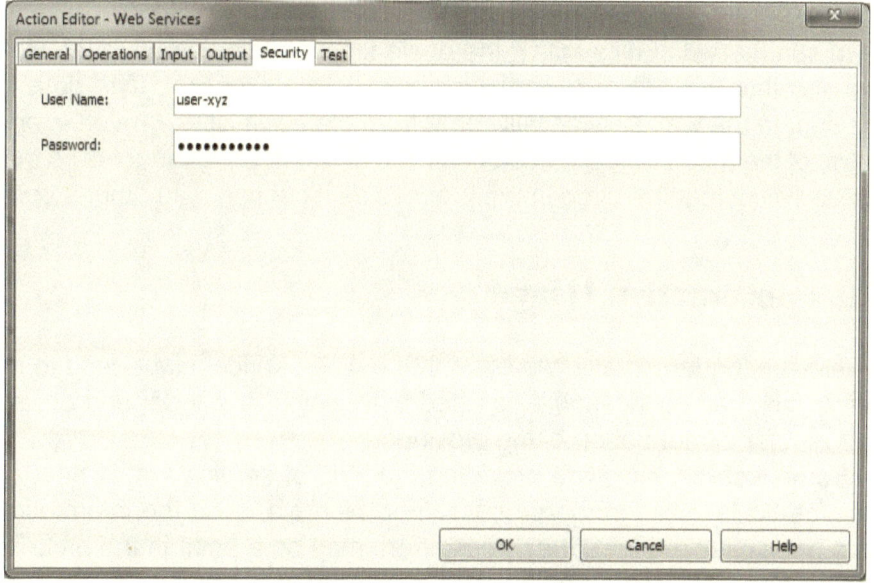

Finally, purely for convenience of the developer, there is a test function that will allow a direct request to be made, and display the results of the request

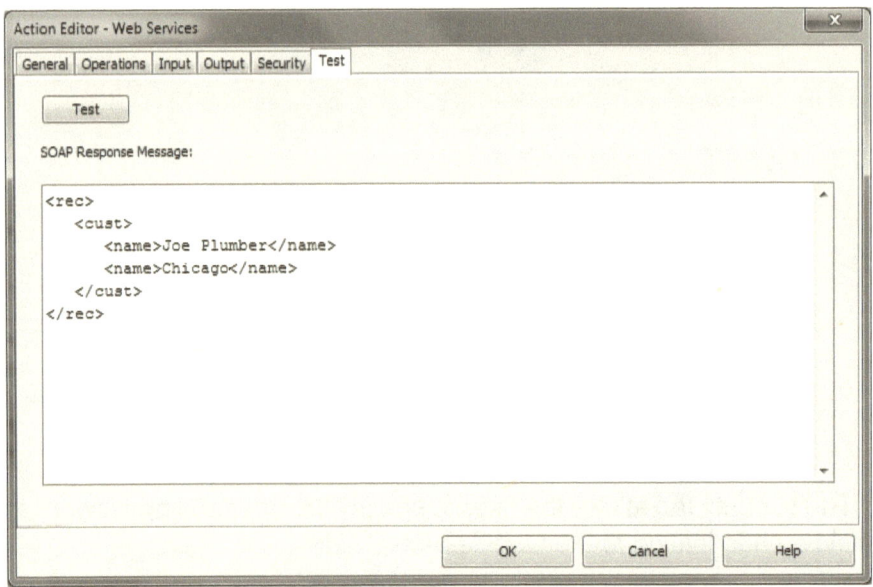

In summary, in Fujitsu DXP the designer is building a call to the web service that will run at a particular point in the process. The data to be sent to the web service will come from the BPM UDA varaibles, and parts of the result will be placed back into different UDA variables so that these values can be used in the process as it continues to other steps.

10.4 Interactive Usage

There are fundamentally two ways that a web service might need to be used. (Not all services will be used both ways. It will depend on the nature of the information being provided.)

Some web services are providing the kind of service that is needed at a particular point in the process. For example, once the information has been checked for correctness, there may be a point in the process where the data values are officially submitted to a service for recoding or transmission. This kind of service must, by its nature, be done exactly once in a process. Once it is done, the state of the process is different, and the user should not be in a place to do it again.

Other web services provide information look up capability. It is conceivable that the user will enter a value, search for records. If none are found, the user might modify the value and search again. There is no limit on the number of times that a user will want to use this in a given process, since the results of one search tell whether to continue searching or not. This kind of interactive behavior might be allowed at one point in the process, but it is not performed as part of the process moving forward. This kind of service is accessed directly from the UI using asynchronous java script style calls which then populate the page with the result as the user does this.

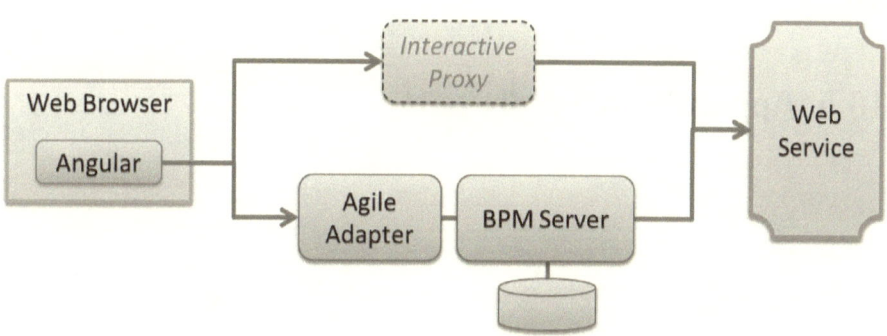

This diagram depicts the two paths. The user interface in the web browser will display the process instance information and allow the user to interact with it. When the user complets an activity, an information post through the Agile Adapter instructs the BPM server to move forward. The process might make any number of web service calls at that time.

The other path is through a module which is called here "Interactive Proxy." This proxy would not be needed in most IT environments, but in Revenu Quebec the web services are constructed in such a way that they can only be called from servers. In order to allow the user to have an interactive behavior to a web service, this Interactive Proxy is a server side component that can access the server, and will do so directly in response to the user's need for information.

The Interactive Proxy does not exist at the time of writing. The requirement is that this server can accept ReST style HTTP requests calls from the browser, and then, acting as a server with a specific well known identity, take the data and submit it as a well formed SOAP request. This step will probably translate from JSON to XML. Then, when the response comes from the web service, the response data will be transformed from XML to JSON, and send all the way back to the browser that requested it. Errors and failures will need to be handled in a suitable manner.

The Interactive Proxy could be implemented in a number of different technologies: node.js, JBoss Java, or other options. The requirements are quite clear: conform to whatever requirements exist that apply to programs that are allowed to call web services, and to present to the browser a straight forward ReST style interface to invoke those web services.

It is not clear if this is a permanent solution, or a transitional solution until the web service providers can provide interactive web services directly.

10.5 Appendix A Wsdl

```
<?xml version="1.0" encoding="UTF-8"?>
<wsdl:definitions name="ServiceRelationAffairesClient" xmlns:wsa="http://schemas.xmlsoap.org/ws/2004/08/addressing"
xmlns:wsaw="http://www.w3.org/2006/05/addressing/wsdl" xmlns:wsa10="http://www.w3.org/2005/08/addressing"
xmlns:tns="http://www.revenuquebec.ca/ws/DossierClient/RelationAffairesClient/2016/06"
xmlns:soapenc="http://schemas.xmlsoap.org/soap/encoding/" xmlns:soap12="http://schemas.xmlsoap.org/wsdl/soap12/"
xmlns:wsu="http://docs.oasis-open.org/wss/2004/01/oasis-200401-wss-wssecurity-utility-1.0.xsd"
xmlns:soap="http://schemas.xmlsoap.org/wsdl/soap/" xmlns:xsd="http://www.w3.org/2001/XMLSchema"
xmlns:wsp="http://schemas.xmlsoap.org/ws/2004/09/policy" xmlns:msce="http://schemas.microsoft.com/ws/2005/12/wsdl/contract"
xmlns:wsap="http://schemas.xmlsoap.org/ws/2004/08/addressing/policy"
xmlns:wsx="http://schemas.xmlsoap.org/ws/2004/09/mex" xmlns:wsam="http://www.w3.org/2007/05/addressing/metadata"
xmlns:wsdl="http://schemas.xmlsoap.org/wsdl/"
targetNamespace="http://www.revenuquebec.ca/ws/DossierClient/RelationAffairesClient/2016/06">
    <wsp:Policy wsu:Id="OSEEC_EP_policy">
        <wsp:ExactlyOne>
            <wsp:All>
                <http:NegotiateAuthentication xmlns:http="http://schemas.microsoft.com/ws/06/2004/policy/http"/>
            </wsp:All>
        </wsp:ExactlyOne>
    </wsp:Policy>
    <wsdl:types>
        <xs:schema targetNamespace="http://www.revenuquebec.ca/ws/DossierClient/RelationAffairesClient/2016/06"
xmlns:xs="http://www.w3.org/2001/XMLSchema" elementFormDefault="qualified">
            <xs:import namespace="http://www.revenuquebec.ca/xmlns/DossierClient/RelationAffairesClient/2016/06"/>
            <xs:element name="ObtenirListeRelationsAffairesClient">
                <xs:complexType>
                    <xs:sequence>
                        <xs:element type="tns:ListeRelationsAffairesRequest" name="CriteresObtention" nillable="true" minOccurs="0"/>
                    </xs:sequence>
                </xs:complexType>
            </xs:element>
            <xs:complexType name="ListeRelationsAffairesRequest">
                <xs:sequence>
                    <xs:element type="q1:CodeIdentifiantReference" name="CodeIdentifiantReference"
xmlns:q1="http://www.revenuquebec.ca/xmlns/DossierClient/RelationAffairesClient/2016/06"/>
                    <xs:element type="q2:CodeTypeClient" name="CodeTypeClient"
xmlns:q2="http://www.revenuquebec.ca/xmlns/DossierClient/RelationAffairesClient/2016/06"/>
                    <xs:element type="q3:ListeCodeCategorieDossier" name="CodesCategorieDossier" nillable="true" minOccurs="0"
xmlns:q3="http://www.revenuquebec.ca/xmlns/DossierClient/RelationAffairesClient/2016/06"/>
                    <xs:element type="q4:ListeCodeLienInterDossier" name="CodesLienInterDossier" nillable="true" minOccurs="0"
xmlns:q4="http://www.revenuquebec.ca/xmlns/DossierClient/RelationAffairesClient/2016/06"/>
                    <xs:element type="q5:ListeCodeTypeDossier" name="CodesTypeDossier" nillable="true" minOccurs="0"
xmlns:q5="http://www.revenuquebec.ca/xmlns/DossierClient/RelationAffairesClient/2016/06"/>
                    <xs:element type="xs:string" name="ValeurIdentifiantReference" nillable="true"/>
                </xs:sequence>
            </xs:complexType>
            <xs:element type="tns:ListeRelationsAffairesRequest" name="ListeRelationsAffairesRequest" nillable="true"/>
            <xs:element name="ObtenirListeRelationsAffairesClientResponse">
                <xs:complexType>
                    <xs:sequence>
                        <xs:element type="q6:ListeRelationAffairesClient" name="ObtenirListeRelationsAffairesClientResult" nillable="true"
minOccurs="0"
```

To see the entire WSDL visit this page: http://appu-systcontribintpes.prod.mr◼

Glossary

ACM solution – A collection of templates created on adaptive case management (ACM) technology designed to meet the needs of a business unit. You can think of this as an "application" to meet a need.

activity – A description of a piece of work that forms one logical step within a process. It is the basic unit of work within a process. Presumably work could be subdivided into units smaller than a given activity, but it is not meaningful for the organization to track the work to that level of detail. Synonyms include goal, step, and task.

adaptive case management (ACM) – An approach to managing work and teams centered around gathering and organizing the information needed for knowledge workers to accomplish goals, without a strong focus on enforcing a process. ACM differs from business process management (BPM) in that the case information is the focus and the thing around which the other artifacts are organized. And it is the case information that persists for the long term. ACM differs from BPM in that BPM has a focus on process and it uses the process as an organizing paradigm around which data, roles, and communication are organized. In ACM, process models are usually not prepared in advance, but instead are assembled on the fly for particular situations.

adaptive case management system (ACMS) – A productive system that deploys not only the organization and process structure, but becomes the system of record for the business data entities and content involved. All processes are completely transparent as per access authorization, and fully auditable. It enables non-technical business users in virtual organizations to seamlessly create/consolidate structured and unstructured processes from basic predefined business entities, content, social interactions, and business rules. It moves the process knowledge gathering from the template analysis/modeling/ simulation phase into the process execution phase in the lifecycle. It collects actionable knowledge—without an intermediate analysis phase—based on process patterns created by business users. An ACMS differs from a BPMS in that the case information is the focus and the thing around which the other artifacts are organized, and that case information persists for the long term.

ad hoc process – An ad-hoc process is a custom process defined in a one-off way. This term should only be used when the process is actually defined and designed in advanced. It is different from an emergent process, which arises out of a collaboration of people with no single person in charge.

agile methodology – To move quickly and lightly. In reference to solution development, it is a method where many short iterations are used, with many quick (internal) releases, so that the nontechnical customer of a solution can be more actively involved in guiding the course of development. The agile approach to development is known to produce solutions that better meet the needs of the customer, and it also allows for greater responsiveness to external changes in requirements.

analytics – A mechanism for collecting and processing statistics in a meaningful way. Process analytics will gather and process statistics about the work in such a way that it is useful for evaluating how well the process is running.

best practice – An approach to achieving an outcome that is believed to be more effective than any other approach under certain conditions or circumstances.

business operations platform (BOP) – A next-generation technology platform oriented toward continuously designing, executing, monitoring, changing, and optimizing critical business processes.

business process – A set of one or more linked activities which collectively realize a business objective or policy goal, normally within the context of an organizational structure defining functional roles and relationships.

business process execution language (BPEL) – A standard executable language, based on XML, for describing a process that uses web service calls to communicate with the outside world.

business process management (BPM) – The discipline to model, automate, execute, control, measure, and optimize the flows of business activities that span the enterprise's systems, employees, customers, and partners within and beyond the enterprise boundaries.

business process management suite/software/system (BPMS) – A software system designed to support business process management. The acronym BPMS is used to distinguish the technology product from the management practice of BPM.

business process modeling notation (BPMN) – A standard set of graphical shapes and conventions with associated meanings that can be used in modeling a business process.

business process orientation (BPO) – A concept that suggests that organizations could enhance their overall performance by viewing all the activities as linked together into a process that ultimately produces goods or services.

business rules engine (BRE) – A software system for managing and evaluating a complex set of rules in a business processing environment. A business rule is a small piece of logic that is separated from the application logic so that it may be managed separately from the application code. Rules are often expressed in a language that is more accessible to non-programmers.

case – The name given to the specific situation, set of circumstances, or initiative that requires a set of actions to achieve an acceptable outcome or objective. Each case has a subject that is the focus of the actions—such as a person, a lawsuit, or an insurance claim— and is driven by the evolving circumstances of the subject.

case folder – Contains all of the case information and processes, and it coordinates communications necessary to accomplish the goal for a case. A case folder can contain information of any type including documents, images, video, etc. Also known as a case file.

case management – A method or practice of coordinating work by organizing all of the relevant information into one place—called a case. The case becomes the focal point for assessing the situation, initiating activities and processes, and keeping a history record of what has transpired. Beyond this generic definition, case management has more focused meanings in the medical care, legal, and social services fields. For this book, we see case management as a technique that could be used in any field of human endeavor.

case owner/case manager – A person who is responsible for the outcome of a case. The case owner can change any aspect of a case and is actively involved in achieving the goals of the case.

case team – The complete set of all people who are involved in a case at any level of engagement. Case team members do work on the case which is coordinated by the case manager.

commercial off-the-shelf (COTS) – Describes software or hardware products that are ready-made and available for sale to the general public. This term is used to distinguish such products from custom software and hardware made specifically for a purpose that is presumed to be more expensive to produce and maintain.

creativity – The ability to transcend traditional ideas, rules, patterns, relationships, or the like, and to create meaningful new ideas, forms, methods, interpretations, etc.; originality, progressiveness, or imagination.

customer relationship management (CRM) – Technology to manage a company's interactions with customers and sales prospects.

design by doing – The concept that the steps to complete a process are designed as an integral part of doing the work itself. This is the opposite of the concept of a *design phase* that is distinct from a *run time* phase. The worker simply does the work, and the process steps are captured by the system automatically.

developer/programmer – Someone with skills in creating IT software applications. We distinguish between the knowledge workers with responsibility for the outcome of a particular case, and the developers who help create capabilities within a case management system. Their relationship to the case, and the responsibilities within the case, are different.

emergent process – A process that is not predictable. Emergent processes have a sensitive dependence upon external factors outside of the control of the process context, which is why they cannot be fixed according to their internal state. Workers involved in an emergent process will experience it as planning and working alternately or at the same time, such that the plan is evolved as the work evolves. Synonyms include ad hoc process and unstructured process.

enlightenment bias – The tendency to believe that behind every phenomenon is a simpler formula or rule that predicts it. Enlightenment bias is the inappropriate use of reductionism.

enterprise content management (ECM) – Strategies, methods, and tools used to capture, manage, store, preserve, and deliver content and documents related to organizational processes. ECM strategies and tools allow the management of an organization's unstructured information, wherever that information exists.

enterprise resource planning (ERP) – Computer system used to manage resources including tangible assets, financial resources, materials, and human resources.

expert – A person who has special skill or knowledge in some particular field; specialist; authority: a language expert; possessing special skill or knowledge; trained by practice; skillful or skilled (often followed by in or at): an expert driver; to be expert at driving a car.

goal – A statement or definition of what is to be accomplished. Functionally equivalent to a task, activity or step—goals can be tasks and tasks can be goals—however a goal is usually considered to be a higher level with focus on the end result and omitting details on how to accomplish the goal.

innovation – A new idea, device, or method; the act or process of introducing new ideas, devices, or methods; something new or different introduced; the act of innovating; introduction of new things or methods.

knowledge work – A type of work where the course of events is decided on a case-by-case basis. It normally requires a person with detailed knowledge who can weigh many factors and anticipate potential outcomes to determine the course for a specific case. Knowledge work almost always involves an emergent process.

knowledge worker – A person with a high degree of expertise, education, or experience, and the primary purpose of their job involves the creation, distribution, or application of knowledge. Knowledge workers do not necessarily work in knowledge intensive industries.

knowledge worker for hire – Someone who is trained in a specific field and learns to be an expert but has little or no ownership of the overall process. A car mechanic must make accurate suggestions on how to repair the car but does not take responsibility for the repair shop business and must work within the constraints set by others.

knowledge worker for innovation – Someone who can plan and be responsible for the course of events. This is defined by Peter Drucker as someone "knowing more about their job than anyone else in the organization." These are the workers who handle the wicked problems and have to think outside of the box, and they have the authority to actually promote and adopt innovative practices (e.g. a board member, entrepreneur, business person, sales person, lawyer, detective, etc.).

lifecycle – This book uses lifecycle only in regard to the work of creating a solution. The development lifecycle of a solution might start with a definition of requirements, development of a process definition, development of forms, testing, deployment of the solution into production, use of the solution by many people, and finally the shutting down of the solution. The lifecycle of a solution may involve monitoring the running process instances and improving those process definitions over time. Note: A solution has a lifecycle that takes it from start to finish; a case has a process or processes that take it from start to finish.

model – A simplified summary or abstraction of reality designed to aid further study. In the business process field, a process model is a simplified or complete process definition created to study the proposed process before execution time.

online transaction processing (OLTP) – A class of systems where time-sensitive, transaction-related data are processed immediately and are always kept current.

organizational agility – That quality of an organization associated with sensing opportunity or threat, prioritizing its potential responses, and acting efficiently and effectively.

predictive analytics – A method of analyzing the work that has been going on, producing from that models of how things are proceeding, and then using those models to predict how things might go a short time in the future. For example, monitoring the patterns of orders made in the morning, along with some knowledge of how long orders take to fill, one might be able to predict how many people will need to stay that evening overtime to get it all complete.

predictable process – A process that is repeatable and is run the same way a number of times. Synonyms include definable process, repeatable process, and structured process.

process definition – A representation of a business process in a form that supports automated manipulation, such as modeling or enactment by a process management system. The process definition consists of a network of activities and their relationships, criteria to indicate the start and termination of the process, and information about the individual activities such as participants, associated IT applications, and data. Synonyms include process diagram and workflow.

process diagram – A visual explanation of a process definition. Synonyms include process definition, process model, process map, and process flowchart.

process flowchart – See process diagram.

process instance – A data structure that represents an instance of a running process. It has associated context information that can be used and manipulated by the process. A process instance plays a role in a business process management suite (BPMS) that is very similar to but not exactly the same as a case in a case management system. A case may have more than one process instance associated with it.

process model – A simplified or complete process definition created to study the proposed process before execution time. Synonyms include process diagram.

programmer – See developer.

records management – Management of the information created, received, and maintained as evidence and information by an organization in pursuance of legal obligations or in the transaction of business.

reductionism – The practice of analyzing the behavior of an entire system as a product of the behavior of its components.

role – An association of a user or users with a set of responsibilities in a specified context. In this case, responsibility means the expectation to perform activities for that context.

routine work – Work that is predictable and usually repeatable. Its predictability allows routine work to be planned to a large extent before the work is started. As the name implies, routine work is considered normal, regular, and not exceptional.

scientific management – An early twentieth century school of management that aimed to improve the physical efficiency of an individual worker by carefully recording precisely what must be done for a particular task, then training workers to replicate that precisely. It is based on the work of Frederick Winslow Taylor (1856–1915).

SCRUM – An agile software development methodology emphasizing iteration and incremental development.

service-oriented architecture (SOA) – An approach to system design where the software functionality is deployed to a specific logical location (a service) and programs requiring that software functionality make use of communications protocols to access the service remotely. SOA has often been discussed together with business process management (BPM), but this connection is coincidental. While BPM might benefit from SOA the way that any program/system would, there is no inherent connection between managing business processes and the system architecture that supports them.

social software – A class of software systems that allows users to communicate, collaborate, and interact in many flexible ways. Generally, such software allows users to form their own relationships with other users and then exchange messages, write notes, and share media in different ways.

solution – A package of artifacts (configurations, forms, process definitions, templates, and information) that have been prepared in advance to help users address kinds of recurring situations. A solution may embody best practices for a particular kind of situation.

step – See activity.

straight-through processing (STP) – The practice of completely automating a process and eliminating all manual human tasks. This term is typically used in the financial industry.

subject (of a case) – An entity that is the focus of actions performed in the context of a case. For example, a person, a lawsuit, or an insurance claim.

task – See goal.

template – The general concept of something that is prepared in advance approximately for a particular purpose with the anticipation that it will be modified during use to more exactly fit the situation. A process template does not define a process in the way that a process definition does.

unstructured process – See emergent process.

work – Exertion or effort directed to produce or accomplish something. Organizations exist to achieve goals and work is the means to achieve those goals. The smallest recorded unit of work is an activity. Activities are combined into procedures and processes.

workflow – The automation of a business process, in whole or part, during which documents, information, or tasks are passed from one participant to another for action according to a set of procedural rules. Synonyms include process definition.

Also from Purple Hills books:

This is a book for couples, with skills and ideas from a 60 year, successful, happy, sexy, marriage. It's about making your relationship work well so that you both feel connected, loved, and supported. Your relationship begins with interest in each other and then builds with love and passion. You want to bond forever.

Bea and Jim Strickland, President Couple of Better Marriages in Silicon Valley, led retreats and Marriage Enrichment groups for 40 years. Jim Strickland was the engineer type with IBM for 32 years. Bea taught communication skills for couples and parents. Touchy, feely. So much in love but with such different personalities. They made it work because they wanted to be happy — fitting together. They learned to fit their differences together and teach others how to do it, too.

http://PurpleHillsBooks.com/

Also from Purple Hills books:

After tens of thousands of years, religion continues to be pervasive. A comprehensive cognitive theory of religion remains lacking as academics cannot agree if religion is an accidental byproduct or an evolved adaptation. Darwin's Apple proposes a new hypothesis for the origin and purpose of religion that finally explains how religion is adaptive and why it endures, even in our rational, modern society.

http://PurpleHillsBooks.com/

Also from Purple Hills books:

When
**THINKING
MATTERS**
in the Workplace

How executives and leaders of knowledge work teams can
take best advantage of technology for case management

Keith D. Swenson & Jim Farris

"When Thinking Matters in the Workplace" is an in-depth review of how knowledge workers and innovators get their work done. It gives you the background of complex organizational behavior and matches that up with mature management approaches as well as business architecture. Then, it surveys the different kinds of technologies you might use to help innovators collaborate and get their work done. Naive approaches can lead down paths that actually make it harder for knowledge workers to get things done. Care must be taken to provide support that increases their productivity. This book provides some guidelines to help avoid the worst pitfalls and to take the best advantage of an adaptive approach for supporting knowledge workers.

This book shows how a case management approach can be applied in almost any field where knowledge workers are needed.

http://PurpleHillsBooks.com/

Also from Purple Hills books:

By closely examining the inner workings of the mind, Mr. Watts exposes the ego-based myths that serve as obstacles to resolving conflicts and to finding happiness and meaning in a polarized world.

With uncommon insight, the author explains how the root of society's and the individual's problems lies in the human mind rather than in social or economic conditions. Based on the exaggerated awareness of separation and differences, rather than of unity and similarities, our dualistic thinking brain totally accepts one side while rejecting the other.

The authentic Self is seen by the author as the key to realizing human potential and to experiencing the greatest high, the love connection between Self and Other that puts the missing piece in place and provides the profound sense of belonging that we all seek.

http://PurpleHillsBooks.com/

Index